Saying ⅃es

to **LIFE** In

Spite of

Everything!

How to prioritise progression and avoid
stagnation

AMY GUDUZA

ISBN-13: 9798721558245

'Life cannot deny itself to the person who gives life their all. If you're serious about changing your life, you'll do something about it. If you're not, you'll find an excuse'.

JEN SINCERO.

TABLE OF CONTENTS

PREFACE

A mother's love is a special gift, a bond that many would consider to be unbreakable; yet my whole life I felt like a bond between my mother and I was never formed. Growing up within a Christian household has not always been the most delightful experience. But, despite the experiences within my immediate environment, I have been able to discover my true identity and pave my own path to freedom - freedom from depression, amongst other things.

My mother's willingness to sacrifice everything all in the name of God led to the neglect of her own children. Not only have I experienced both financial and emotional deprivation, but I have continuously witnessed my mum use God as a justification for her irrational actions – actions that have once led to us being homeless.

For a very long time, I questioned whether my own mother loved me or whether she was even capable of loving her child. This is not to say that my mother did everything

1

wrong, because much of her parenting was great. There was order in our household, despite being raised without my father.

My mum disciplined my siblings and I very well and ensured that we had a good routine, which enabled us to obtain good habits that have benefited us thus far. However, the times that were out of control, were such that it left me with the overall impression that I was not loved.

The constant manipulation, dictatorship, and disregard of my feelings and well-being resulted in a turn for the worst in my mental state. I never valued family until recently, as the resource of love and trust was depleted; thus, resulting in a loss of relational and emotional energy.

Instead of home being a place that I could run to, it became a place that I used to run from. Alcohol and weed were the two things that provided an escape for me, but I soon realized that that route would only lead to a dead end.

There came a time in my life where I no longer wanted to feel internally empty, but instead wanted to be better and do better.

Just as one moment has the ability to bring despair, it also holds the potential to lead to a powerful new beginning. That same moment that has the ability to ruin us also has the power to preserve us. In the midst of the transition from pain to a new beginning is hope. I had hope that things would get better, that I would get better.

What you will read in these pages is ultimately an account of that hope manifested into reality. This account will caption my transition from using what would be deemed to be 'worldly' measures to escape my reality, to seeking liberation through Christ, which then allowed me to create a new reality. One where love, peace, and joy remained at the centre of my being.

My personal experiences with my mum left me with one question: what beauty will I create with the space that she has left me with? Instead of continuously looking at her and her actions, I shifted my focus and began delving deep within myself. I analysed my character, my beliefs, my thoughts, my actions and my reactions. I had a part to play in the change that I wanted to see.

I look back at my life and I barely recognise the person that I was in the past. My mindset has shifted to a completely different dimension and I have been able to embrace pain whilst continuously moving forward - and you can too.

The changes that I have witnessed within myself and the experiences that I have encountered - both good and bad - have inspired me to write this book. Everyone has a story to tell and I have found the courage to tell mine.

The first part of this book, Gracefully Broken, is the personal account of my life experiences. Most of the characters within this section of the book remain a part of my life, albeit in varying degrees. What has changed, of course, is the context in which the book might now be read. For those of you reading this that may have met some of the people within this account, I hope not to change your views towards them but rather for you to gain an insight into my perspective and the encounter that I have had with those individuals.

For the thousands of nameless children who have felt as unworthy of love as I have - this section is for you.

The second part of this book relates directly to the title of this book - Saying Yes to Life in Spite of Everything. Here I will focus on the importance of prioritising progression and how to do so, in order to avoid remaining stagnant.

The space between pain and wholeness deserves your undivided attention and this section of the book will help you fill that space.

I will touch upon practising stillness, and how it can be both beneficial and harmful depending on when and how you use it. I will touch base on how seasons of darkness hold the potential to change your life and I will provide you with tips on how to move through those seasons. I will also delve deep into the importance of correctly rooting yourself and how becoming rooted will require you to be both patient and intentional.

This section of the book will provide practical steps that I have used in my life journey, that have helped me to say 'yes to life in spite of everything'. These steps will enable you to embrace pain whilst continuously moving and will shine light to the fact that the decision to keep on moving forward, despite what is thrown your way, all comes down to YOU. You have a choice to make and I hope this book will be a stepping stone in enabling you to make that choice.

I believe that there is always the possibility of changing your reality and creating the life that you have always dreamt of living. No matter your experiences in life, or the family that you are born into, you have the ability to blossom and achieve all that you desire to achieve.

My goal is to help young people help themselves, and one of the ways in which I believe that this can come into fruition is through a change in ones' mindset and internal state.

I aim to instil hope into the hopeless as I believe that there are no hopeless situations, but rather, there are individuals who think hopelessly.

PART ONE

GRACEFULLY BROKEN

Fear not for I am with you,

be not dismayed for I am your God,

I will strengthen you, I will help you, I will uphold you with

my righteous right hand.

(Isaiah 41:10).

One

MY PARENTS AND I

My mother is from Zimbabwe and is a loving and caring woman at her purest form, but above all, she is devoted - to Christ. For as long as I can recall, my mum has been a member of the Christian domain and ensured that my sister and I were also brought up within the church from a very young age. I was raised by my mother alone, and I have to give her the appreciation that she deserves because being a single mum is not easy. My mum ensured that my siblings and I grew up with a good routine. We were given time to play, time to study and time to do our chores. She really did try her best and I have reaped the rewards of her efforts.

If there is one thing I can say that I have learned from my mum, it is to always be myself and to remain true to who I am.

From a very young age, she reinforced the idea of natural beauty to me. She encouraged me to see myself the same way that God viewed me - a child that has been wonderfully and fearfully made (Psalm 139:14). If she were to do a hairstyle on me that I didn't like, she would always tell me that I looked beautiful. The same goes for when I would leave my natural hair out and not like it - she would tell me yet again, that I am beautiful, and I think this is important, especially in a society where 'beauty' has been defined to look a certain type of way. The constant obsession of a lifestyle that is manufactured through careful selection, displaying only what can be perceived as perfection, has led individuals to compromise their self-worth, and in some instances have led to alterations in individuals' appearances in order to 'fit in'.

What we learn about ourselves and the world around us is influenced by family, and I think it is important for every child to be encouraged by their family to love every part of themselves - my mum saw to it that my siblings and I were comfortable in our skin. My mum was intentional about making sure that we cared less about other people's opinions and more about how we saw ourselves.

Another trait that my mum holds is that she wants to do good in life. Much of her time is spent evangelising and encouraging individuals to give their life to Christ. She would sometimes spend hours talking to random people on the streets, listening to their life journey and spreading words of encouragement. She spends hours praying for people, even for those who have done wrong against her and she so often encourages me to do the same. Parts of her actions have proven her to be selfless, but other parts have proven her to be selfish.

Every parent has to make decisions, most of which will come with sacrifices, but what matters is whether those decisions are for the greater good of those involved. Although I know that my mum is a loving person at her purest form, one thing I cannot ignore is that some of the most crucial decisions that she made, were not made out of love.

As much as being devoted to Christ can be a good thing, what I have experienced through my mother's devotion hasn't all been good.

You see, my mum has not always been a Christian, but many years ago she encountered a dream which led her to give her life to Christ. She dreamt of a specific church with a specific Pastor and she made it her aim to find that church. And so she did.

The church that she attended was called Gilbert Deya Ministries, and once she started attending this church, she became so involved in the ministry that she practically gave her whole life to it. My sister and I were quite young when my mum began taking us to church services with her - I was four years old and my sister was six years old - and my mum would regularly take us to night services, which would run throughout the night to the early morning the next day. It was during these services where we were exposed to things that I believe children should not be exposed to at such a young age. Things such as people falling on the floor, rolling around screaming, bodies shaking and much more.

Whilst my mum was attending this church, she would regularly give an offering (a contribution of money to the church) or she would sow a seed (a sum of money that is often a larger amount than an offering).

This is not to say that there is anything wrong with sowing a seed, because as children of God we have been called to be givers, but my mum would often give amounts that were above her means. She believed that she would be blessed if she were to sow a seed and to give all that she had. This is another trait that my mum has - she is a giver.

They say that charity starts at home, but I always felt as though charity began elsewhere for her – the Christian community. Unfortunately for us, this habitual behaviour (of giving beyond her means) resulted in us becoming homeless, thus leaving us with one option - to sleep in the church, so that is what we did.

To date, I am still unaware as to how this situation got resolved, and with whose help; but I know that my eldest sister was definitely a part of the process, as she had to come down from university to be of assistance, and eventually we were given back the council house.

That is as much as I know, as whenever I tried to talk to my mum about something that happened in the past, she so often dismissed me and refused to engage in the conversation; instead, she would say: "what happened in the past must stay in the past". This particular trait is what has made is so difficult to build a relationship with her, as she would conceal a lot.

Most of what you will read within the next coming pages will shine light to my past relationship with my mum - or lack thereof.

My Dad, on the other hand, has always been more willing to talk about the past. However, I am unaware as to whether that is because he felt as though he owed it to me to do so, due to his absence in my life, or whether it's because he took pride in all that he accomplished in his past.

Whilst growing up I had a lot of resentment towards my Dad, partly because I never understood why he wasn't a part of my life and I always questioned whether things would have been easier if he were around to offer a helping hand. I didn't really know much about my dad when I was young and I was never really interested in getting to know him.

My mum would always encourage me to speak to him and to encourage him to come and stay with us here in London, as he lived in South Africa, but I never had that desire. I didn't think it was my place to encourage my dad to come and live with us as I was the child and he the parent. If he wanted to be here, then he would have been. It was his responsibility as a parent to take interest in the lives of his children and I have never felt like he took interest in mine.

However, as I got older I made the conscious decision to speak to him a bit more often so that I could understand his life journey and his reasons for making the decisions that he made. I began to understand his interests, beliefs and character.

My Dad is a proud South African man who takes pleasure in ensuring that others are aware of the Guduza name (my surname) and the weight (the accomplishments and struggles of those associated with that name) that it carries - so much so that he puts himself first. Most of my engagements with him have revolved around much of his accomplishments.

He had a story to tell for every situation and as much as I have enjoyed a lot of his stories, I had also hoped for him to take a bit more interest in my life. I had hoped for him to be intentional about building that father-daughter relationship. But, the more I became aware of his character, the more unlikely that was of happening.

He would rather continuously admit that he has lacked responsibility as a father to me, than to act toward changing the current status of our relationship - or lack thereof. The only time I have felt him take interest in my life was when I graduated from university. He was proud of me for all that I had accomplished and saw to it that others were aware of my achievements. He even came to London for my graduation ceremony. That is something that I really appreciated.

My Dad is an intelligent individual with strong political interests, but he is more concerned with serving his country than being present in the lives of his family members. He is a great example of what inner strength entails, as he has battled a lot throughout the course of his life.

At the age of 20, he became a ZIPRA (Zimbabwe People's Revolutionary Army) soldier, which is just one snippet of the many other experiences he has encountered. Both him and my mum came here to the UK in 1986 as refugees - they were survivors of the Gukurahundi genocide and their journey here was far from smooth sailing.

My dad has played a huge role in enabling my family members to start a life here in Britain and for that I commend him; however, he has lacked complete and utter responsibility as a father to some of my siblings and me.

He is a father to 8 biological children and 2 adopted children, and although I can't speak much about the role that he has played in the lives of my siblings, what I can say is that his absence was most definitely felt by me.

This is not to say that my Dad doesn't love his children, I don't doubt that he does, but it is something that I've heard him tell me, more than show me. For me, actions speak louder than words, but I understand that for some, showing love comes easier to them than it does to others. I am also aware of the fact that some of his experiences may have affected his ability to show affection; however, to try is better than to do nothing and I have witnessed my dad do nothing more times than I have witnessed him try.

Despite all of this, I am thankful that I at least know who my father is and have access to him, as I know that many people have been robbed of the opportunity to meet their fathers.

My parents' journey started off well. It is a shame that they grew apart as I came into the picture, however, irrespective of my experiences with them, I love them both unconditionally.

The experience that I am about to share with you in the next section begins from about the age of 15. That is when things got real for me. As I invite you on this journey with me, you will unravel the current status of my relationship with my parents.

Two

HOME

My home was a place that I would call: 'a home of arguments'. It wasn't somewhere that I would run to if I were facing problems elsewhere, instead, it was somewhere that I used to run from to escape the problems. The environment of my house was hostile and it was quite lonely as we had never done anything as a family.

I am 1 of 8 siblings, but 1 of 4 from my mum and dad, with me being the last-born child. I lived with my sister Sharon, my sister Fikile and my brother Nkosi.

I didn't really have a strong relationship with any member of my family, apart from my older sister Fikile, and when she left for University I felt like I was alone. She wasn't at home during the experience that I am about to share with you.

There's only a two-year gap between my sister and I and we grew up doing everything together. I always felt as though I could tell her anything, yet there were many things that I went through that I didn't tell her about - all of which you will unravel throughout the course of this book. In hindsight, it probably would have benefited me if I had told her because she could have helped me get through it, but instead, I decided to go through everything alone.

If you have good people around you that you trust, confide in them. They are there for a reason and may be willing to help you unpack your burdens within a shorter time period.

It was a struggle to be heard within my house and I found myself engaging in a constant battle with myself – a battle to find and maintain inner peace. Once I had gained that peace, I had to really fight to keep it, as I was living in an environment where my peace was constantly compromised. It is only now that I have learnt that it is your inner state that determines your experiences and not the other way around.

The depth of the hostility of my home will unfold within the next three chapters of this book.

In 2013, my dad came to London for some hospital appointments as he was severely ill.

My mum was always happy when my dad came as she would associate his return with the 'restoration' of their marriage. The one thing she has always prayed for, is for the restoration of their marriage. She believed that God told her that their marriage would be restored and that is what prevented her from divorcing my dad many years ago. So, every time my dad came to London, she would fill herself up with the hope that this time he was coming for good. She believed that God had brought him back for a reason and that her prayers were being answered. Did my dad ever stay for good? No. He always went back to South Africa. I would always try to warn her beforehand that he is going back to his home, but she would always say *"Don't speak like that, have faith"*; but what she didn't understand is that I couldn't have faith in something that I didn't believe in. I did not believe that the idea of the restoration of their marriage was from God, and quite frankly I did not want to play happy families as this was not a happy family.

Anyhow, on the day that my dad was leaving my mum couldn't even bring herself to come and say goodbye to him, so she just stayed in her room until he had gone.

Once he had left I saw her getting ready and asked her where she was going. She told me she was going for a walk, and it was at that moment that I knew that his departure had destroyed her. Her hopes had been shattered but she didn't want to face the reality of it. Instead, she kept on believing that one day he will be back for good. When she arrived home from her walk her eyes were red, so it was evident that she had been crying. I asked her what happened, but I didn't expect her to tell me as she never does. Surprisingly, this time she did. She came to me and told me she went to a park and just sat by a tree and wept. My heart sank to my stomach. Seeing my mum that upset was painful to witness. She deserved to feel loved, to be happy, and to be free.

Having to continuously see my mum pick herself up and then drop back to rock bottom again was a hard pill to swallow. Even now, I am still yet to see pure happiness when I look at her. The only time I would ever really see my mum happy was when my Dad would come, and the only time she would really try to be with us or even fully provide for us (in terms of buying food), was when my Dad was here.

There were many things that I never quite understood and I had so many questions. One being - why she would put her vision of her and my dad being together, and likewise the church, before the well-being of her children.

After my Dad had returned to South Africa, things got worse at home. My mum became radical in her walk with Christ. She had stopped signing on for job seekers allowance (a benefit provided to those who are not in full-time employment yet are capable of working and are actively seeking employment) and had thus stopped paying the bills.

My siblings and I were unaware of this at the time and months later we realised what was happening, as my mum started receiving letters from the housing association, informing us of our eviction date. Prior to that, my mum had already missed the court date which none of us were even aware of. She believed that God had instructed her to do this and that he would show up and save our house, saying "God is in control."

All of this was happening when I was 15 going on 16,

during my final year of secondary school, whilst I was preparing to take my GCSE's. My free school meals had been stopped due to my mum refusing to sign on for job seekers allowance which meant that I wasn't being fed properly. I lost so much weight during this period and I remember people constantly mentioning it to me, but I just used to change the conversation as quickly as possible. It was hard enough dealing with everything going on at home alongside people constantly telling me that I have lost weight as if I didn't notice it myself.

My siblings and I tried so hard to persuade my mum to start paying the bills. We had discussions almost every night, most of which would go on until 4 a.m. in the morning. I would spend the whole night trying to fight my case to my own mother and she would dismiss me and just say *"Go to bed, you have school in the morning."*

We tried everything, we wrote letters to the housing association, and my older brother and I even went to visit them in person so that we could explain the situation and ask for an extension on the eviction deadline. We even went to desperate measures and got a Pastor from my mum's church to come to our house, because we truly believed that the only person that my mum would listen to at this point would be a Pastor. She refused to accept advice from anyone who she deemed to be in a lower position of authority than herself, hence the constant dismissal of my views.

It was impossible to be heard within my household. It was either my mum's way or the high way.

There were times where she would be shouting, and I would just look at her and think this isn't my mum, it was as if something came over her and she lost all control and consciousness. Her actions became very unpredictable. During this whole eviction period, my relationship with my mum was the worst it had ever been. I remember one day I opened my eyes in the middle of the night and she was just standing beside me in my room at 4 a.m., praying over me. This was because she believed I was against her, when in fact, I wasn't. She would automatically see a disagreement as an attack.

I have always wanted and will always want, what is best for my mum and our household; but, I just didn't agree with her actions and the decisions she made. She had none of our best interests at heart. If I were to oppose something that she said, she would then go on to say that the enemy (the Devil) was using me. At one point I even laughed because I couldn't believe she thought the enemy was using me. She would even walk around my room with a handkerchief that was anointed by an American pastor who she has followed for a very long time - and if she wasn't using his handkerchief, then she would be putting his anointing oil on my head or around my room.

She would constantly receive letters of invitation to his conference in America, which would reassure my mum that her attendance would guarantee her breakthrough. I can tell you now that I do not believe in a prayer of breakthrough. You decide when you want to break forth! Everything has been made available to us, God gave us dominion over the world, and it is up to us to put the word to work (Genesis 1:26-28; Luke 10:19; Psalm 8:6).

My mum wasn't working at the time, yet she would always manage to find a way to pay for a ticket to go to America, in order to attend this Pastor's conference (I have decided not include the name of the Pastor in order to avoid the risk of any judgement being made against him). I couldn't believe that my mum was always willing to pay to attend a religious conference in America, yet she was not willing to pay the bills to ensure that her children remain sheltered. Instead, she was willing to sacrifice everything all in the name of God! A God that I do not believe told my mum to do this.

My mum always believed that her attendance was not only for her good but for the good of every family member. She would justify her actions through the use of the bible, however, she was making the mistake of not taking the word of God for what it is, but instead, she would manipulate it to be the way that she wanted it to be. If I were to bring another scripture before her, that opposed what she was doing, she would dismiss me and say, *"That is not the scripture I am talking about."* It was all about her. She would not even acknowledge what I was trying to tell her.

Below are a few examples of the things she would say, or shall I say, shout:

"SHUT YOUR MOUTH!"

"I AM THE RIGHTEOUSNESS OF CHRIST."

"GET OUT! THE ENEMY IS USING MY CHILDREN, I COMMAND YOU TO GET OUT!"

"YOU ARE JUST A CHILD, YOU DON'T HAVE SPIRITUAL UNDERSTANDING."

"YOU CAN'T SEE INTO THE SPIRITUAL REALM."

"I AM GOD."

There are many examples I could give, but the list would be endless. Moreover, I begged my mum not to do this to me, I cried to her endlessly and all she did was look at me with a blank face. She would sit there and watch me cry and not care. She had no emotions whatsoever. I always used to ask her why she didn't care and why she was putting me through this, especially because she knew how much I wanted to excel in my studies.

My older brother, Nkosi, once said to her, "*Your youngest daughter is crying to you mum; can't you see that?*" and she didn't respond.

These months were the worst and most difficult months of my life and it made me question whether my own mother loved me.

The one person I thought I could rely on had failed me. I had hope that she would be able to show me that she loved me or that she cared but my hopes were shattered. I honestly was not asking for much.

All I asked of her, was for her to pay the bills so that I could complete my exams in peace.

Even though my household wasn't a peaceful one, I would come home and keep to myself. I would just go to my room as soon as I got home and do my own thing. It was one thing having to deal with not feeling like your worthy of being loved or worthy of being cared for, but it was another thing losing your mum and home in the process.

Moreover, whilst all of this was going on, I began having panic attacks regularly. I used to clench onto my duvets as a way of dealing with them so that I could fully focus on something in order to get my breath back.

Eventually, I began getting them regularly, but I didn't tell anyone about it, I just dealt with it myself. It never crossed my mind to go to the doctors because I just thought that they would eventually go, but they got worse. I began getting up to twelve panic attacks per week. I would go to school every day, work as hard as ever, put a smile on my face and be the bubbly person that I was.

However, eventually one day in school I had the biggest panic attack and collapsed. I was called in for a meeting and had no choice but to tell them what was going on, as they had also noticed that I was no longer on free school meals. The first thing that they said to me was that they were going to have to call social services, but I begged them not to. My relationship with my mum was already fragile and I was so sure that this would make it even worse.

However, in their defence, my health and wellbeing were their top priority and to them, my mother was viewed as someone unstable and incapable of looking after me properly, so they went ahead with the call. As much as I didn't want them to at the time, I am glad that they got social services involved as my social worker was a huge help. I had regular visits from my social worker and she topped up my free school meals allowance weekly so that I could get food.

During one of the visits, she sat me and my mum down together and she gave me two options: it was either I go into foster care or move in with a family member. My mum heard this and said nothing. I had hope that maybe, just maybe, reality would hit her and that she would change her mind and sort out the housing situation, but I was wrong yet again. She continued to refuse to sign on for job seekers allowance and instead left it in my hands to decide what I wanted to do.

There was this one day that I will never forget, where my mum broke down to my social worker crying and begging her for help. I remember her saying she wanted her own social worker and that she didn't know what was going on with her. I immediately began to weep. I was crying because my mum was crying and even though she had placed so much emotional pain on me, she was also in a dark place and had not spoken to anyone about it.

Throughout all of this not once did I think about what she was going through or how she was truly feeling. I was so focused on how she was hurting me that I was oblivious to the fact that she was hurting. She didn't even understand what was going on with her. Thinking about that day breaks my heart because I remember it so clearly and the emotions were high.

My mum was just broken, and her world was falling apart right in front of her without her even realising it. It wasn't possible for her to get a social worker of course, but my social worker had regular talks with her and suggested counselling. Meanwhile, I had a decision to make regarding where I was going to stay, so I got in contact with my Aunty and she was more than happy to take me in. I was only able to move in with a family member who was a home owner, so my aunty was pretty much my only option. I remember the day we were all leaving the house, my brother Nkosi moved into his flat in Central London and my other sister Sharon had ordered a delivery van to move her stuff into her flat. I had packed up my room and one of my friends came to help me move everything to my aunt's house.

We dragged most of my things onto the bus as we had no other means of getting there, but thankfully my aunt's house wasn't too far from mine. As I was leaving, I hugged my mum and she left me with two words - ***"Take care."*** That one line has stayed with me until this day, forming my biggest life lesson: **DO NOT RELY ON ANYONE BUT GOD**. She actually let me leave. She let me go without a fight. It happened. That experience completely changed my life.

To date, I do not believe that what happened was from

God because what my mum was doing and the way that she acted, opposed the characteristics of Christ. God is all loving and her actions were not from a place of love. Instead, I believe that my mum's actions were self-inflicted, and this is why it is so important to distinguish between your own actions and your obedience to God. There are many individuals out there who make their own decisions and then use God as a justification for their actions.

This was by far one of the most hurtful and painful experiences of my life to date, but also the one that has shaped me into the person I am today.

It was a powerful experience as it taught me that no one in this world is obliged to give you their time, effort, or love. I rely on absolutely no one but God, because if the woman who held me in her stomach for nine months could let me go without a fight then so could anybody in this world. One scripture that got me through was Deuteronomy 31:6 – *be strong and courageous. Do not be afraid because of them, for the Lord your God goes with you; he will never leave nor forsake you.*

Just to be clear, within that particular moment of time, my mum was not in her right state of mind and was clearly going through severe depression. Therefore, I can't deny the possibility of her having acted differently if she had been in a different state.

Moreover, my siblings and I had all moved out of the house, but my mum remained, as she refused to leave until the day of the eviction. I remember going back to the house once with my cousin as I had left my bike there, and upon arrival, the house just looked dull and pretty much empty.

There was absolutely no food in the house, apart from expired milk so I was wondering how my mum had been surviving. I went upstairs to her room and knocked on her door but got no response. So, I knocked again saying "*mum*", but still didn't receive a response. At this point, my heart was beating fast and I was imagining the worst, so I rushed in there praying that she hadn't done anything to herself and I saw my mum sitting in the dark staring at the wall. The curtains hadn't even been opened and the lights were off. I kept saying "*mum... mum... hello... mum.*" I even waved my hand in front of her eyes and got no response.

Do you know how heart-breaking it is to see your own mother like this? Never in my life did I ever think that things would get this bad. I don't think any words are enough to describe how I was feeling on this day. It felt like I didn't even know who that woman was, or rather, she didn't know who I was.

To date, mine and my mother's relationship is still a working progress, but it has improved drastically. Whilst this was going on, my siblings and I were still trying everything to get an extension on the eviction date. We tried everything within our means - I literally mean everything. We explained the whole situation in full, from my mum's depression and unresponsiveness, to social services involvement, etc. We did not give up without a fight because I couldn't live with my aunty permanently and I was not willing to move into a foster home...that was the last thing that I wanted. With time, we eventually got given an extension on the deadline and further down the line my mum agreed to turn the situation around.

My social worker played a huge role and I am forever grateful. My mum still wasn't in a good state, but after having an assessment she was put on anti-depressants and attended group counselling.

Whilst this whole housing situation was taking place, I began smoking weed. We were due to be evicted in January 2014 and I remember this so clearly because this was the first year that I entered the new year at a park getting high, whilst watching fireworks instead of being in church and thanking God for seeing me through the year.

For others, smoking weed may mean nothing, just a casual thing, but for me, it was everything. It was much deeper. Not only did it go against all my values in life and my upbringing, but it was also a coping mechanism. It was a way of me escaping my reality and entering a fantasy world.

At the time, I felt like getting high was fun; it made me laugh and I had 'good' experiences from it as well as bad ones. Most times it was just something that kept me calm and helped me fall asleep. It was a distraction as it helped me stop thinking about my life and my home environment.

I remember during the build-up to my GCSE's, I would literally go to the library to revise and then go to the park and get high.

There was one day where I did balloons (for the first time) and smoked weed at the same time and I immediately blacked out. It was as if I had died for a few minutes and then resurrected. I can't even explain what happened because I don't even understand it myself but when I woke up all I could hear was *"Amy...Amy...Amy."* It all felt like a dream. My face started to go pale and I couldn't move! I literally could not stand. My friend was so high she couldn't even help me get up, so I literally had to slither to the kitchen to get water. I remember praying that day, asking God to help me and in exchange promising to never smoke again. You would think that an experience like this would stop me from smoking again but believe it or not, it didn't.

That summer I received my GCSE results and I made it into the Grammar school I wanted to go to! I was never one to fall behind on my work and not care about my education.

I worked twice as hard that year because of everything going on, but at the same time, I began doing things that I would never have imagined doing. All I know is that I put my all into those exams, and I was in the library more than ever before, even whilst smoking and drinking.

Although my results were good, that summer was one of the worst summers I have ever had. I started working as soon as I received my NI number, and my first job paid me £3.72 per hour!

Most people would decline the offer, but I didn't hesitate to accept it. I did not complain. In fact, I was happy that I got a job because, for me, it was all about surviving. If I didn't fend for myself then who would? I didn't care what others thought - I had to earn some sort of income that would get me through. I knew I was starting Sixth Form, so

I worked long shifts, eleven hours a day most times, just so that I could buy everything I needed for Sixth Form. I was also very lucky to have older siblings that were willing to help me out here and there or lend me money until I could afford to pay them back.

That summer of 2014 was also the summer that I fell into depression. I was no longer the happy and bubbly person that I usually was and it was the first time that I began getting annoyed at myself because I couldn't keep it together. I really struggled to bring myself out of a pit of sadness. There were nights where I would cry and cry and cry and didn't even know why I was crying. I was 16 at the time and I would find myself just staring at the wall in my bedroom, crying. I would be up for hours and most nights were sleepless nights for me. I remember telling one of my friends that I think I have depression, and she responded with *"Nah you don't. Trust me."* That response just reinforced the feeling of loneliness and made it seem even more real than it was. It was at that point, that I had made up my mind to get through whatever comes my way alone. The feeling of sadness escalated, I was barely eating or talking to people and couldn't seem to figure out how to get myself out of that situation, so I eventually went to the doctors about it. I can hands down say that I HATED my life. I didn't want to live anymore. I used to imagine dying on a daily basis.

I had regular appointments with the doctors and the first thing they would ask me is whether I had suicidal thoughts. I would sit there for a minute before answering, and then I would reply: "no". I would lie not only to the doctors but also to myself so that I could hang in there for as long as possible. They eventually put me on anti-depressants alongside referring me to counselling.

Nothing helped me. I was tired, like genuinely tired. Tired of life, tired of living, tired of all the tears, tired of the lonely days, tired of everything. At this point, I don't even think I was religious anymore. I questioned the whole idea of religion. I grew up in a Christian household and went to church every Sunday, but I had stopped going to church by this stage. I always questioned God. I always asked: If God was real, then why would he put me this through this? Why would he watch me go through this and not help? Why was this happening to me?

Three

THE BEGINNING OF FREEDOM

My sixth form experience was a special one. I attended Dartford Grammar School for Girls Sixth Form and I met some of the most amazing individuals. These girls never failed to correct me if I were to do something that was out of character. They showed up for me daily and never failed to remind me that I didn't have to go through things alone. I didn't even have to tell them anything specific, yet they kept on reassuring me that whenever I was ready to talk, they would be there and that was more than enough for me.

I enjoyed my time there, for the most part, but the atmosphere of the sixth form was quite competitive from time to time. It felt as if it were a dog eat dog system. A lot of people there were very much stuck in their ways. I was so glad that I got accepted into a grammar school, but it was far from what I expected it to be like. The jump from

GCSE to A-levels was big, but the move from a comprehensive school to a grammar school was another jump within itself. It was the first time I was thrown into an environment where I was in such close proximity with people from privileged backgrounds.

This not only made me more protective of myself, but it also made me aware of the fact that I had to work twice as hard just to get to where I needed to be. The teachers were no better than the teachers within a comprehensive school. In fact, a lot of them didn't even have a clue what they were doing. You were expected to carry your own workload and get through it and so that is what I did.

Within my first week of Sixth Form, September 2014, I began having debates with people about life and about God. I remember there was one thing I said that stood out to my friend Ife, which was: *"What if we are just puppets living in this world, being controlled by other people; like what if nothing is actually real." "For all I know God might not even be real."* As soon as Ife heard this, she stepped in and responded with: *"Nah Amy I'm bringing the bible in, we're going to discuss this."* My thoughts were wild! I didn't believe in God within that current moment of time and in fact, I actually blamed God for a lot of things that were going wrong in my life. But, as I sat down with Ife and spoke to her more, my thoughts were challenged.

Ife was not only committed to understanding me as a person and my journey, but she was also committed to helping me know and understand the truth. She introduced me to the greatest gift in life, which is Christ and that is why

I am so eager to take the gospel to the nations because Christ SAVED me.

Aforementioned, I used to imagine dying but this got worse during Sixth Form. For example, if I was sat in one of the balconies of the assembly hall, I would just imagine myself jumping off. I can't stress how important it is to control your thoughts because they can lead to your next action (Proverbs 4:23). If you are ever presented with the opportunity to help someone, do it. If you have a word for someone, give them that word, because speaking from experience, I have seen how one word can go a long way for another person.

Gradually, I began to let Ife into my life and I would tell her things that I hadn't told anyone before and she was always willing to sit with me and listen to me, and then advise me accordingly. I think the most amazing part is that she was willing to walk through everything with me. One thing that she helped me understand is that *'we fight not against flesh but against principalities and powers'* (Ephesians 6:12).

I began to understand the principle of seeing with your spiritual eyes and not physical eyes, just like when God told Abraham that *'as far as your eyes can see, that which I have given to you'* (Genesis 13:14). I was eager to know more of the word of God so that I could live by it and so I started listening to podcasts and reading the bible more often. There was this one day where Ife sent me a song called Identity by James Fortune, and when I listened to this song I found myself weeping before God.

I didn't understand why I was crying but I found myself asking God to change my identity. I no longer wanted to live the way that I was living and for the first time ever I felt surrounded by love. I could feel the warmth of Christ around me, I felt protected and covered. One song gave me that feeling. This was the first time I had experienced love at this magnitude.

Marianne Williamson says, in her book a return to love, that *'one sincere surrendered moment is when love matters more than anything and we know that nothing else really matters at all'* - this was the moment where **love mattered**. It felt as though something was telling me that it's okay to let it all go - all the baggage, all the pain, all the hurt - to release it all. For the first time in a long time, I felt as though I wasn't alone and that I had never been alone. A higher power greater than me had been watching over me throughout the last couple of years - that higher power was God. It was through that one song that I decided to dedicate my life to Christ and became saved.

That song broke chains for me. The lyrics of that song were pierced into my heart and from that day onwards, I was so dedicated and committed to change. I listened to a podcast every single day and I used every opportunity that I could to listen to the word of God. Whether it was during a free period at sixth form or during my bus journey home. I never listened to a podcast without taking notes, and all the notes I took, I stuck on my wall in my bedroom. If anyone were to walk into my room, the first thing they would see were my walls covered in notes. I was surrounded by the word of God. I wanted to go deeper. I wanted to change. I became tunnel vision after my encounter with God. I had the desire to know and to understand God on a deeper level. I went from a place of seeing God as the reason as to why my family was falling apart, to seeing God as my healer, my restorer, my 'ever-present help in times of need' (Psalm 46:1). That one experience that initially brought me pain, was the same experience that preserved me.

If you want something to change in your life, you must consciously make the decision to take actions that are going to lead you towards that change. It all comes down to how hungry you are for change.

That year I grew so much spiritually, and I realised that God first chose me before I chose him. I knew I had to let go of certain things in order to truly live the life that God had called me to live, but this was much easier said than done. It was a struggle, to say the least.

One thing I struggled to give up was smoking. It was hard for me to stop smoking weed because I was surrounded by people who were also partaking in that activity. I would find myself smoking during the week and even making plans to go and get high on a Sunday after church and despite all of this, God still loved me! He did not leave nor forsake me - there was no condemnation. He said to 'come as you are', so I came as I was.

The more that I listened to the word of God, the more I realised that the identity that I had in Christ was different to the one that I was portraying to the rest of the world, so

I had to stop. I had to stop surrounding myself with certain people and had to let go of a lot of things in order to be fully devoted to my walk with Christ. There was shedding and there was a splitting. I was so stubborn and stuck in my ways, but the more that I drew closer to God the more I heard from him and his instructions became so clear to me that I had to obey.

One thing that I have learnt is that **you are as close to God as you choose to be.** Yes, he first chose us before we chose him, but we are in control of our spiritual journey. We are responsible for our own progression. It took me ten months to completely stop smoking without relapsing, but once I had stopped, I felt a change within myself.

The way that it happened was so beautiful. I was in church one day and my Pastor was calling people who felt as though they had deteriorated in their walk with Christ to come to the front. Anyone who wanted to rededicate their lives to God were called to come to the alter. All of a sudden, my feet just started walking to the front and I found myself pouring my heart out on the altar.

Ever since that day, I have not smoked weed and do not intend on doing so ever again. It has been six years since I gave my life to Christ, and it has been the best journey I have embarked on thus far.

My attendance at sixth form was not the best. I missed a lot of days at sixth form and received criticism from all angles. My teachers would constantly doubt my ability to get into university due to the number of days of sixth form that I had missed. However, what they didn't understand was that I was fighting other battles of my own that I chose not to tell them about.

Here I was trying to escape a toxic environment at home, only to attend another one that was equally as toxic. Despite the number of days at sixth form that I had missed, I prevailed and made it into the university that I hoped to attend. God's grace was sufficient.

Sixth Form was the beginning of a cutting away for me. A rebirthing season. I said yes to Christ and no to the world. **What are you willing to say yes to no matter how hard it may appear to be?**

Four

UNIVERSITY

First year of University was one hell of a rocky journey for me but it was also one of the greatest years of my life. It was the beginning of something new. Something fresh. One of the first things I did upon my arrival was apply for jobs. Working has always been non-negotiable for me as I have been left with no choice but to fend for myself. One thing I can say, regarding getting a job, is that God has always had my back! I never struggled to find employment and I am forever grateful for that. God's mercy really does endure forever, and **he will forever meet you at your point of need.**

My first job at university was at Topshop, and although I was given a four-hour contract, I would usually work around twenty hours per week. It was quite hard trying to balance working whilst meeting the demands of higher education, as well as trying to maintain a social life, but by the grace of God, I made it through. One month into university I found out that my Dad was coming to London, so I decided to go and see him one weekend in October 2016.

Prior to my arrival, my mum had already informed me that we were all going to be having a family meeting, but I refused to attend as I was no longer willing to engage in the same pointless discussions that we had year after year. I was no longer willing to waste my time and energy having discussions with people who made decisions that only benefited them. I was no longer willing to stay up until 6 a.m., having the same pointless discussions that never led to a solution.

I had already made up my mind that I was coming home solely to see my dad and to do a late birthday celebration with my friends from London. So, the rest of the family went ahead and discussed without me…… but this time I was completely wrong. The meeting was not an argument or a debate, but instead, it was a family gathering put in place to inform us of my dad's illness. I was due to return back to Southampton that same weekend and as I was packing my bags and getting ready to leave, my sister approached me and informed me of my dad's several illnesses (of which I have decided not to state, as I do not think it is my place to do so).

For the first time ever, I felt my heart sink to my stomach. I could not believe it. To say that my mind was scattered would be an understatement. My initial response was to put gospel music on and continue packing. It was only when I was on the coach back to Southampton that it hit me. All that kept going through my mind was: *just as I thought things were about to get better, they just got worse.* I used my first week back in Southampton to spend time in God's presence and to delve deep into his word. This really stirred my spirit and for the first time ever I understood the importance of interceding on behalf of others. This journey called life is not just about us, it is about others. **Life lies on the other side of service.** You see my dad was an atheist and had always been, so if I didn't pray for him then who would? I do truly believe that to date, God has kept him - and I will unravel more of this belief throughout.

Three months into University, I started having thoughts regarding whether the University of Southampton was a good fit for me. I wasn't sure as to whether this was because I found Southampton boring, or whether it was because I believed that I was putting myself into debt when my family were already financially unstable. I wasn't sleeping properly, I wasn't eating properly, and I couldn't stop thinking! I spoke to some of my family and friends about it and they told me to just continue with university and see how I feel by the end of the year, so I did.

I stopped working for three months and decided to use that time to get in touch with myself. I read books, I journaled, I spent more time in God's presence, I travelled, and I seized every opportunity that came my way. For example, I started looking online for opportunities that would allow me to be a part of something that was bigger than myself. Through searching and putting myself out there, I managed to secure a fully funded 3-week social enterprise venture that took place in Mumbai, India. This was just one of the ways in which I seized the opportunities that I came across.

I was eager to get out of my head and to step into the present moment. I had a vision of the life that I wanted to live - one where freedom, internal peace and love remained at the centre of my being. I wanted to really make the most out of the life that I had been given and wanted to take a hold of my internal state, so that my peace would not be moved by my external circumstances. I was ready to begin my journey of bringing that vision into fruition. I had made up my mind to give life my best shot and to create the life that I had always dreamt of living.

My time spent with God enabled me to grow and develop into the person he had called me to be. Now, this is not to say that I didn't face any challenges during that year, because I did, but one thing that you must learn to accept is that the challenges will never stop. I had accepted that life will surprise me with things along the way but that shouldn't stop me from doing what I want to do. The Bible tells us to '*count it all joy when you go through trials and tribulations, for the testing of your faith produces patience, but let patience have its perfect work, that you may be perfect and complete, lacking nothing*' (James 1:2-8). So, whenever I was faced with trials, I would keep on pushing through because I knew that '*all things work together for good, to those who love God and are called according to his purpose*' (Romans 8:28). As I went throughout the year I longed for a Godly community. I wanted to meet more people in Christ – people who could hold me accountable and I could hold them accountable – and towards the end of the year, I crossed paths with those people. This was one of the things that contributed to my decision to stay in Southampton.

I passed my first year of university with an upper second class, which I was quite pleased with and that same year I also set myself a goal to travel to twenty different countries in the space of three years. I always wanted to travel the world and seeing as I had just committed to doing more of what I wanted to do, it seemed like the perfect time to start. So that same year I flew to Spain, Morocco, India, and Italy!

Although by the end of my three years at university I hadn't met my goal of visiting twenty countries, I managed to visit twelve countries and fifteen cities, which was a huge accomplishment for me as I always thought that people like me didn't get to do things like that, but I managed to do it!

I accomplished this mainly through working, as at certain points I would be working at more than once place. I also applied for opportunities that paid me and I used some of the money that I received as a bursary from my university. It just goes to show that **with God by your side, the right mentality and the willingness to put in the work, anything is possible.** If you want something in life, go out there and get it. Be a go-getter!

Letting Go and Letting God

After having such a great summer, I was determined to make my second year of university a great one. During my first month in, I decided not to go on social media and instead I spent a lot of time working, reading books, watching ted talks and applying for internships. I said my positive affirmations daily and was just pretty much in the headspace that I had hoped to be in.

In October 2017, I went to Milan for my 20th birthday, which was amazing but, in all honesty, I wasn't actually happy on the day of my birthday. I had just turned 20 and my phone broke that night, and to top that off, my mum forgot it was my birthday. I called her to tell her that my phone was broken and that's when she said: *'oh yeah it's your birthday'*; so, she only remembered because I mentioned it - how sad. In addition to that, this was the first time ever that I thought my dad would message me, as I had been in constant communication with him, but no that didn't happen. Disappointment again.

The only person who remembered was my sister Fikile, whom, aforementioned, I am very close with. My older sister also messaged me right at the end of the day, my brother didn't message me as he had cut all ties with me the previous year.

It felt like my life was really coming together this year but at the same time, there were many aspects of my life that were falling apart. One aspect being my family. Not in a million years did I think one of my siblings would cut me off but because of my past experiences, I was able to move on. Life continues with or without people.

Anyhow, that year at University, I was determined to find more people in Christ, so I started attending a Christian society which held a bible study session every week. The week after my birthday, the topic was: *'Who is the father?'* We were asked to write down what came to mind when we thought of our earthly father and what came to mind when we thought of our heavenly father.

When I had to write down what I thought about my dad, the first thing that came to my mind was 'useless', but I must explain why I wrote that. At that point in time, I was annoyed. I was annoyed that I was making more effort with him than he was with me. I was annoyed at the fact that he would ignore my messages and reply whenever it best suited him. But most of all I was annoyed at the fact that he couldn't even bother to wish me a happy birthday. I thought, after 19 years it was the least he could do. However, when I had to write down what I thought of my heavenly father, I had so many positive things to say such as: He is my life, the very reason I breathe, my happiness, my joy and my strength. He is caring, loving, never failing and much more; but most of all, He is enough.

God is the only person that has and always will be there for me through everything. It was no coincidence that the day after this bible study I received a message from my dad, which read:

"Hi Amy. Happy belated my sweet girl. I am so sorry for being an unhelpful father to you and all the others, but my love for all of you is beyond reproach. I love you all very, very much. This is not the platform to address all your questions, perhaps I will try by email. For

*now, please kindly note that I together with junior and his mother
survived a nasty car accident a week ago in which the car was damaged
beyond repair, a complete write-off. All the best Dad."*

Having received this message, I felt the need to meditate
upon the scripture that reads *'Love is **patient**, love is kind, love
does not boil nor envy, love **does not hold onto past wrongs**,
it is not self-seeking, it does not rejoice at injustice but rejoices with the
truth. Love bears all things, believes all things, hopes all things and
endures all things'* (1 Corinthians 13:4). The two parts that
God told me to focus on was that love is patient and love
does not hold onto past wrongs. He told me that I should
be patient with my parents, that I will have that relationship
with my mum that I have always longed for, but I just need
to hold on. Love is kind, meaning that no matter how I am
treated I should show kindness. That I shouldn't respond
with anger but respond with love. That I shouldn't consider
all the past hurt, all the disappointments, and that I should
stand firm on the word of God, knowing that I will see the
promises of the Lord in the land of the living.

Believing that my relationship with my mum will be
restored is one thing, but actually holding onto that vision
through EVERYTHING was beyond tough. The hardest
part was waiting period, especially because that mother-
daughter relationship was something that I had longed for
all my life. However, one thing I learned through the
process was to act whilst waiting. For example, even during
the waiting period, I would constantly seek more wisdom
and knowledge through different means. I would read
books that would add to my personal development. I would

talk to different people who may have gone through similar experiences to mine. I would listen to a variety of podcasts and sermons, all of which would add to my knowledge and then I would apply it to my daily life. The part of the scripture that touched me the most in 1 Corinthians 13:4, is where it says *'love endures all things',* because I have truly been through it all with my mum, but I do not want to lose hope.

I love my mum with all my heart, and I want nothing more than for her to be truly happy and to live the life that she deserves and has been called to live. She has been through a lot in her life and I want her to live a life full of joy and happiness; a prosperous life - one that God has called each and every one of us to live, as he takes pleasure in the prosperity of his children (Psalms 35:27).

Moreover, during the month of November, God truly started working on me and revealing things to me that I would never have expected. It was one of my toughest months of 2017 but one of my greatest months, purely because I had experienced spiritual growth. I was so hungry for more of God, and more of his word. I wanted to be so deeply rooted in his word so that I live by it daily. I wanted my first response to challenges to be the word of God. The word before my emotions.

I remember there was one day I got back from work and suddenly, my heart became heavy. I started crying and then my mum just came into my mind and I started weeping. I had an urge to call her because something was not sitting right in my spirit. So, I called her and asked her what's wrong, and she replied *"Nothing, everything is fine"*, but I didn't believe her so I responded saying: *"Mum I know something is wrong because I can feel it"* and that's when she told me that she didn't want me to worry and that I should just focus on my studies because she wants me to do well.

But, I couldn't focus on my education when deep down inside I knew something was wrong, so she eventually ended up telling me that she was facing her own trials and that she had stopped signing on for jobseeker's allowance - again! This meant she was no longer paying the bills as she wasn't receiving any income and was instead living for God and God alone. She believed that God had called her to do his works, which in her eyes meant that she should sacrifice everything and just work for God. I couldn't believe this was happening AGAIN! I honestly thought we had passed this for good but clearly not.

Once I had come off the phone to her I thought about what I should do but deep down inside I knew that there wasn't much I could do. I went to work the next morning, continued seeking God, checking up on my mum and doing my assignments. I think through it all, what frightened me the most was the possibility of her experiencing depression again and that was something that I wanted to avoid as that was one of the worst experiences of my life.

November was tough for me because I was reminded of everything that had already happened and confronted with the possibility of it all happening again. I spoke to my mum a few times to try and talk sense into her, but she was so adamant - she had already made up her mind and nothing that anyone could say or do would make her change her decision. She continued proclaiming *"This is what God has told me to do and I must obey"*, but I didn't believe it was from God. I believe that she made her own decision and then used God as a justification, yet again. She always talks about how God has done things for other people so why wouldn't he do it for her.

One person in the bible who she always referred to was Job. Job was stripped of everything and was then blessed with more. However, my mum's situation was completely different - this was self-inflicted. I asked myself, over and over again, why I kept on trying to help someone who clearly did not want to be helped, but no matter how much I wanted to just walk away and leave her be, I couldn't. If I were to give up on my mum, I would be giving up on everything that I have ever longed for. That's how I felt. If there were anyone who could persuade my mum to rethink her decisions, or anyone that she would at least open up to, it would be me.

Despite my many attempts to let go, I never have because at the end of the day you only get one mother and one father and there is a reason as to why God chose me to be her daughter and her to be my mother. I love my mum so much and I want her to experience my love whilst here on earth, because if there is one thing I have learnt, it is that life is too short. **Learn to find and keep a hold of gratitude even within the midst of a storm and to find joy in the small things.**

December approached quickly, which meant that Christmas was near. I had never been one to get excited about Christmas approaching as quite frankly the whole idea of spending it at home as a 'family' always made me anxious. During my first year of university, I spent Christmas alone in Southampton, but in my second year, I went home for Christmas as my mum wanted all of the family to be together. My workplace arranged for me to be transferred to a store in London so that I could be home for a longer duration of time and still work.

Upon arrival, I noticed that things at home were really bad. One of the first things I noticed was that my mum was using Daz - the washing powder that is meant for washing clothes - as hand soap! She was also using it as washing up liquid to wash the dishes. I was honestly SHOCKED. I could not believe that it had come to this.

My eldest sister had told me that if she wasn't the one buying things then my mum would literally have nothing, that she would probably be using newspaper as toilet tissue. It was only within that moment that I realised how bad the reality of our situation was. I couldn't believe it. I still can't believe it. Things needed to change.

During my time at home, my sister had informed me that she had spoken to my dad, who informed her that our Grandma was really ill and urged us to come to Zimbabwe as soon as possible to see her. I couldn't afford to buy a flight ticket to Zimbabwe, so my older sister went on behalf of all of us and stayed there for about three weeks.

My mum remained, as she had always been against going back to Africa, for her own reasons – which, until this day, I am not 100% sure of. I know that it is mainly to do with the fact that she believes that many people there are against her. Every time I asked my mum when we would be going back to Zimbabwe, she would always say *"We will go next year"*, and for the past ten years we have not gone back.

Whilst my sister was gone, I was the one buying the food until my other sister arrived from Belgium. I remember there was one day that the heating went off and I had informed my mum and she responded, *"You're going to have to top it up then."* There was never a please or a thank you. I would be getting up at 6 a.m. to go to work and come back to see my mum still sitting in the same position, doing the same thing she was doing before I left: Praying.

This season really taught me to put the word before me, and my emotions behind me, as there were times where I felt as if I could have lost my mind. All she did was pray, read the bible, or go to evangelise. I was tired of witnessing that same routine of hers.

There was one day I was at home and she used my phone to call her mum and all I could hear was my grandma asking my mum when she was going to come to Africa to see her, and my mum responded: *"I will come mum, I will come."* It was a sad moment because I could tell from the way that my grandma was talking, that it was no longer a matter of wanting to see her daughter, but instead, it was a matter of needing to see her.

Two days later, I came home from work and my mum had told me that my grandmother had a mini-stroke and was in the hospital.

The day after, I called my mum to ask her if she was in our local town, as I wanted her to get something for me, but when she answered the phone she was weeping, and when I say weeping, I mean WEEPING. As in, she could barely breathe. I barely ever hear my mum cry, so this broke me. All that kept coming out of my mouth was *"What's wrong?"*, *"What has happened?"* My heart was beating so fast, with so many thoughts rushing through my head. She never told me what was wrong, and we never spoke about it when she got home either. The next day, I went to church with my friend Nadia, and the word was so good that we left there saying *"We are ready for any challenges that come our way."* We were literally screaming *"BRING IT ON."* Aha, little did I know that the challenges were going to come that quick. Nadia stayed at my house the next day, and when we woke up the next morning, my mum came into my room to tell me that my Grandmother had just passed away. Tears started rolling down my eyes. It all felt so surreal.

Within less than a week of her experiencing a mini-stroke, she was gone. My mum had told me not to worry and to just focus on my studies but what she didn't understand was that not everything was about my studies. This wasn't about me. This was about her. I know my mum wanted to be strong in that situation, but the death of her mother hit her hard. She wasn't eating properly after her mum had passed away and she became more radical with her walk in Christ.

On one of the days following her mother's passing, I sat with her in the living room and she started crying. She

52

told me that everyone is against her and I knew then that I had to be the strong one for her. It was sad to see her cry like that, but it was even harder witnessing her grapple with her emotions as she attempted to hold back her tears. I told her to be strong and not to worry about what others are saying about her, but instead to hold onto the memories that she had with her mum and to focus on what lies ahead.

Jesus faced accusations and oppositions left right and centre, but he still rose above it. I reassured her that things would get better in due time and that, at the end of the day, she is the only one who will ever truly know the relationship that she had with her mum, and the memories they shared, so she should just hold onto that.

All that kept going through my mind was that there is no way that God would allow this to happen, two days before the new year, without there being something bigger in store. There must be a bigger purpose to everything we have been through as a family.

New Year's Eve came around quickly and I had the most remarkable entrance into the new year. I entered the new year at church, thanking God for his underserving mercy and for his grace that is always sufficient.

January was a very strange month for me as I just didn't feel like my usual self. I started having panic attacks, which came as a shock to me as the last time I had experienced any panic attacks was three years ago. As they became more regular, I booked myself in for an appointment with my doctor, but she was quite unhelpful as she just gave me breathing techniques to use that I was already aware of. I went home almost every weekend that month in order to catch a break. Midway through February 2018, I suddenly became quiet.

There was a change in my character, that other people had picked up on, before I had noticed it myself. I am usually such a bubbly person, so when I don't speak much people tend to assume that something is wrong.

At the time, I thought that this sudden quietness would be something that would fade away within the next couple of days, but it didn't.

People either kept on asking me what's wrong or telling me that I don't seem like my usual self. I didn't really understand what was going on with me, but what I did know is that I felt like I was being attacked with other people's thoughts concerning my feelings. I didn't even know how I truly felt, yet I started to believe everyone else's opinions regarding my own feelings.

I became so numb that I couldn't feel anything. I would cry without even knowing why I was crying. I would walk to work but not even realise that I was walking to work until I had got there. It was as if my feet were moving ahead of my head. I wasn't in touch with myself at all and I was just constantly drained. I had absolutely no energy to talk to anyone. The only time I would find myself engaging in conversations with people was if I was at work or if I had bumped into someone whilst studying at the library.

That month was a really weird time in my life for me, because although I was still spending time in God's presence, I wasn't actually actively seeking him or his word.

I would listen to a few messages here and there, but I didn't feel complete. It was as if something just wasn't sitting right with me. I started going for walks with God and I would just cry and ask him why I was feeling like this, but there was still no response. I didn't know why this was happening and as much as I tried to come out of it, I couldn't. It was as if I was trapped.

The worst part about this season was that I allowed other people's thoughts to become my thoughts, and as soon as I realised I was doing that, I knew I had to seclude myself. I felt as though I needed a long period of time away from everyone, where it would be just me and God, as the numbness that I was feeling clearly wasn't something that was going to go away within a few days. There were many things that I hadn't dealt with internally, alongside things going on at home that I was battling with, so I knew I had to take the necessary actions to deal with this.

A couple of days later I felt the urge to go back home to London, so I did.

Before heading back to London, I decided to go to Birmingham to visit one of my friends who was studying at university there. We had booked tickets to attend a worship night that was taking place that weekend, but when the weekend came around, I didn't want to attend.

I remember arguing with my friend as I didn't want to go to the worship night, but she couldn't understand why, and neither could I. She was so persistent for me to go, she kept on telling me how it's not like me to not want to attend a worship night and she was right.

I'm not one to miss out on spiritual activities as these are the things I am usually thirsty for, so I didn't understand why I was fighting it...until I got there. So, I ended up going to the worship night and I am glad I did because whilst I was there, God revealed to me (through a song) that the area he wants me to work on is my trust.

God wanted my trust to be without borders - for me to have no limitations or restrictions on how much I trust him. I should trust him wholeheartedly in every area of my life.

The song through which this was revealed to me was Oceans - by Hillsong. So, when I went back home to London, I decided to seek more of him, to make a commitment to myself that even though I felt as though God had distanced himself from me and had gone silent on me, I will not stop digging deeper. I will keep on searching, keep on abiding in him, as *'he is the vine and I am the branch and he who abides in him bears much fruit, for, without him, I can do nothing'* (John 15:4-5). I made a commitment to keep on seeking God until I became moulded into the person he has created me to be. All I can say is that the revelations were truly remarkable. There's nothing more rewarding than seeking more of God.

That season was what I call my 'dry season' as it was a season where I didn't hear Gods voice, until toward the very end of that season. It was a season where I had to feel alone in order to go back to my creator. I had to search for him. You see, **a lot of times we may be waiting on God, but God is actually waiting on us.**

I was hurting but I learned not to reside in my pain. Lisa Nichols once said 'it's okay to be in pain, but don't reside in it. You may walk out of it or crawl out of it, but as long as you stay in consistent movement out of it then you will be fine'. I embraced the season that I was placed in and used it to my advantage. I had just quit my job, and my flesh was battling with my spirit.

Once I was in God's presence it was hard for me to leave it. It was as if he wanted me to stay there. When I wasn't in his presence my mind was thinking about so many things, such as the assignments that I had to do, the housing situation, the fact that I was no longer earning an income, and much more.

My mind started going into overdrive, so it is no surprise that God wanted me to remain in his presence, as that was when I was most peaceful. He wanted me to give it all to him, all of my burdens, all of my struggles, all of it. He wanted all of me. Within that season I unravelled so many scriptures that were specific to particular areas in my life. I knew then that it was time for me to take a hold of the word and fully apply the word to every area of my life. I stopped overthinking my circumstances. I didn't care anymore. All I cared about was going deeper with God. Everything else could come after.

I was reminded of the scripture that says: 'seek first the kingdom of God and then all these things shall be added unto you' (Matthew 6:33). **When you think you have surrendered, surrender more.**

Whilst enduring this season, one of the most vital things I learned was to love the person that you are during vital moments of transition and to love the person you are becoming. I kept on comparing myself to an older version of myself, but I realised that change is bound to happen, so I began embracing the person that I was becoming.

I started to appreciate myself more and to love myself more, as that will set the foundation as to how others should love me. I also learned to guard my heart like never before, as I didn't want my home situation to interfere with the reason as to why I was in London – which was to get back in touch with myself. It was actually one of my friends who told me to guard my heart, as I had asked for her advice.

This is why I say be consciously aware of the people that God puts in your life because you never know how far one word can go for someone. I remember speaking to my mum about the housing situation and her response was: *"If you're unstable here then it's best if you stay in Southampton"*, but what she didn't understand is that everything I was saying to her, was to help her. It wasn't about me, it was all about her.

Being at home was not ideal as it wasn't a peaceful environment to be in. At that time, it was just me and my sister Sharon who lived at home. She had moved back home as she was doing her master's degree. My brother Nkosi would come home occasionally and would often be between his flat and our home. My sister Fikile was in Belgium at that time and came back in May 2018.

I remember there was one day where my brother and my mum were arguing about something, and that argument quickly escalated. I was upstairs working on my assignments and then all of a sudden, I heard shouting that seemed like things were about to get out of control. I ran downstairs to see what was going on and my brother had locked my mum in the living room and was holding the door handle, shouting: "YOU ARE NOT COMING OUT. YOU CAN STAY IN THERE UNTIL YOU SHUT UP." Things were out of control.

What type of household was I living in? Those were my thoughts. I had to keep on telling them both to just drop the conversation and move on, but the arguing didn't stop until my brother eventually walked away. As you can imagine, I was battling with trying to gain peace of mind whilst meeting my deadlines and trying to convince my mum to sign on for jobseekers' allowance, so that she could turn the eviction situation around. It was a lot.

Having remained at home for about three months, I decided to go back to Southampton in May 2018, just before my exams began and during this time, I was still seeking God - not only individually but also, collectively.

I took every opportunity that there was for me to attend a fellowship or a worship event so that I could be surrounded by other fellows in Christ and spend time worshipping together. I felt like during that season there was most definitely a revival.

The most amazing thing about that season was that I experienced God in a fresh way and God started to speak to me through visions as I was worshipping! This is powerful because a starting point of a cry for wisdom is to be consumed in worship (Proverbs 9:10). The starting point of my surrender was found in worship. I remember at my first worship event I saw a vision of clouds above the building, clouds that were full and the scripture that came to me was *'when the clouds be full they shall empty themselves'* (Ecclesiastes 11:3). God had told me that I had entered a new season, one in which I would experience a turnaround! I just kept hearing two things:

1. There's going to be a shift
2. This is your season of a turnaround

I held onto those two things daily. I kept on telling my friends that there was going to be a turnaround and some of them even tapped into it! Whilst walking to places I would keep on saying that there's going to be a shift in my life and that I am about to experience a turnaround.

As I kept going to worship nights I kept on seeing the same vision! Some were more vivid than others and I felt as though God had heard my cry. I believed that the reason as to why the scripture in Ecclesiastes came to me, was because everything I had prayed for was about to be manifested into reality. All those days I spent interceding, praying, crying, worshipping and seeking God had been stored in these clouds and now that the clouds were full, they were about to release the rain - which in this case was the blessings that God had in store.

During the first week of May 2018, I attended a worship event that was held at my university campus. There was a youth pastor who ministered at this event, and during his ministry, he mentioned that he had received three words from the holy spirit which were specific to three different individuals within that room. Little did I know that I would be one of those individuals.

He specifically stated, and I quote: "there is someone in this room who has been going back and forth with their family for years, you haven't had the best relationship with a particular family member for years and now you are about to be removed from your home. God wants you to know that he is restoring your family and restoring that relationship. Don't lose hope." I knew immediately that that individual was me, but I couldn't believe he knew. If God isn't real, then how do you explain something like this? The most amazing thing about this is that that was the same day my mum had received the letter of eviction. God truly does work in mysterious ways.

On this day I was reminded of God's love and of the reality that he is always present. I began to rest in his arms and trust him even more.

One thing I learned is that God is more concerned that you trust him than feel him. Rick Warren states in his book, 'The Purpose Driven Life', that 'true worship begins when your spirit responds to God', and that 'we do not worship to feel good but to do good'. I experienced exactly that within this season. If I remember correctly, it was exactly one week before the eviction date when my mum had changed her mind again! She had decided last minute that she didn't want to lose the house and that she wanted to turn the situation around.

However, this time I wasn't sure whether the housing association would let us off the hook due to the number of times my mum had done this previously, but they did. That month we had gotten a solicitor to work thoroughly through everything and present us with our best options, and the deadline was eventually extended and we were given a court date in August. I was in-between Southampton and London at this point, so I would usually come back to London most weekends.

There was one weekend when I came to London and my mum had told me that Pastor T.D. Jakes was going to be preaching at New Wine Church on the day that I had arrived and that it was the only day that it was free! I immediately knew that I had to go, and I remember saying to my mum that there's going to be a shift. I could feel it with everything in me. I just knew that this service was for me and that there was something huge in store for me, and I was right.

One of the first things that T.D. Jakes said as he got up onto the stage was that there is going to be a shift in this building! I was like "WHATTTTTTT!" I genuinely couldn't believe what I was hearing. He then went on to say that there are clouds above the building! That was it. That was my confirmation right there. I had been seeing visions of clouds above a building for the past two months and God had already told me that there was going to be a shift in my life, so that was all that I needed to hear.

To say that the service was amazing would be an understatement. To say that I received would be an understatement. But let's just say that it was from that day onwards that things changed for me internally.

That was the day that I received a spiritual shift and it is a day that I will never forget. He spoke about the mosaic of Moses, and that the more that you put the pieces together, the better the picture. He touched upon how many of us are mosaics and that at the end we get to see the beauty of what looks like a shattering situation.

God has a strategy whereby all things work together for good and although things may not always seem good, at the end of it you will realise that all those steps were necessary. Only God can put the pieces together in your life. You had to become broken. You had to become shattered so that God could fit you into the right place. Nothing that you went through is without reason. He protected you for a purpose!

When God has something for you, he will make you survive things that you would never have been able to survive on your own.

A month later, June 2018, I had finished my second year of university and I was preparing to go to South Africa alone for six weeks during summer. South Africa had come at the right time as I needed a long break to gather my thoughts and come to terms with all that had happened that year, so I took a twenty-three-hour flight to Cape Town and off I went. Whilst in South Africa, I volunteered in a child and youth care centre, working with girls aged 13 - 18, planning and delivering a women empowerment and life skills program. Working and spending time with these girls was such an honour. Their ability to rise above the difficulties they experienced within their lives at such a young age was touching. South Africa will forever have my heart as it was a stepping stone to freedom for me, or shall I say surrendering.

I have never felt so carefree and happy ever before in my life. For the first time ever, I knew what it felt like to let go and let God. It was during my time in South Africa where I unlearnt and re-learnt how to truly surrender. I took every day as it came and didn't worry about anything.

I met some of the most amazing people out there and I fell in love with my journey. I accepted the person that I was and the person that I was becoming, and I felt closer to God than ever before.

My time in Cape Town was most definitely my season of manifestation. Everything that I had prayed for and longed for started to manifest whilst I was there. The whole experience was just beautiful and truly life-changing. I hiked for the first time ever, I cycled along the coast, I went to my first braai (a South African BBQ) in a township and danced with people I didn't know. I journaled every week, I wrote letters to God and to my future self, and I participated in a walk for freedom on Nelson Mandela's day. I lived, I laughed, and I loved. I felt as free as a bird! I don't think any words could describe accurately what this experience

means to me, but I will leave you with my last journal entry
that was written whilst I was there:

Cape town   *11/08/18*

*So today is my last night in South Africa. My time here is coming
to an end and I still can't believe how quick it has gone. To sum it up
I would say I have learned, I have lived, I have laughed, and I have
LOVED. I can't help but think and feel as though greater things are
coming my way after this. I feel as though God brought me here for a
reason and has strategically planned my steps, especially in regard to
certain individuals whose paths I have crossed. So many people have
been eager to know about my life and at first, I didn't know why but
now I guess it's because each and every one of them had something to
say to me that was going to contribute to my season of a turnaround.
My supervisor and other random people kept on telling me that God
is healing my heart. At first, I didn't understand it as I didn't even
realise that my heart was broken or that there were still broken
wounds, but I guess sometimes it is much harder for us to realise and
see just how broken we are. Sometimes all it takes is for others to see
it for us. Ever since coming here, I have realised just how much of a
blessing I am to others and how much of a blessing people are to me;
but most importantly I have realised that I have a lot to work on in
terms of forgiving my mum. I love her so deeply, but I keep pushing
her away due to the fear of being loved. This is not to say that she
doesn't love me but many times I find myself denying her of the
opportunity to be able to show me. I guess I am scared that if I let her
in and become vulnerable with her then she will hurt me all over again.*

That is what I fear the most, but I must find a way to overcome this fear, so from this day onwards I am making a commitment to myself to put my past behind me and to whole-heartedly give this relationship another chance. I do still believe that until my mum removes her own thorn then she will never fully heal and so neither will our relationship.

Halfway through writing this, my housemate Amrit came and told me that this place is special to me and that my time here is not over. She told me that she can feel and see that I am going to come and do work here, so I shouldn't be sad when I leave as my time here is not completely over. I felt that spiritually. My heart goes out to those girls I worked with and they will forever hold a special place in my heart. I have always had a desire to help others and to instil hope into the hopeless, but it is only now that I have seen just how much hope needs to be restored in individuals. I know that I cannot motivate another individual or empower someone, I can only do my part to help activate their self-motivation.

I am where I belong. I have learnt so much more about the person that I am and the person that I am becoming within the space of six weeks, than I have throughout this year. Change is such a beautiful thing and I am willing to make a habit of being in uncomfortable situations in order to grow, learn and give more of myself away. I no longer have to say, "I can't wait until I am successful", but instead I now say to myself that "I am successful". I have changed my perception of what success is and I know that my future is going to be so bright. I no longer want to entertain certain things or people but instead, I want to commit to fulfilling my purpose more than anything.

I am happy here, peaceful here, free here and present here.

I feel so in touch with myself and so connected to God. I don't want others to interrupt this space. I really want to focus on what matters in life. My life will never remain the same and this is only the beginning of greater things. Trusting Gods timing is the best thing. I am where I am meant to be right now. It is society that tells you that you're behind and that makes you feel like you need to catch up. Focus on your own journey and never let another person's journey steal your joy. No matter what situation I find myself in, I will always focus on the bigger picture. I made a promise to myself a very long time ago that I will always remain grateful and that I would never give up and so far, I have kept that promise and will continue to. For the first time ever, I can hands down say that I am proud of myself. I commend myself for how far I have come because I look at my life and it is barely recognisable. I am thankful for everything that has happened in my life.

Having told Kuselwa about my journey in life, she said something to me that hit me. She said, "it's interesting how other people's actions can force us to change". I couldn't have agreed anymore.

I am happy. I am loved. I am free.

THANK YOU CAPETOWN FOR EVERYTHING. YOU HAVE MY HEART.

Lots of Love,

A.G. XO

Whilst I was in Cape town, my mum attended the court case to do with our eviction (aforementioned, the deadline was extended) and they dropped the case!! I came back from South Africa in good spirits, feeling like a completely different person and many people started to notice it. I was able to uphold positivity, even amid negative situations and I learned to walk through difficult times in a new way, with a new attitude. Things didn't get to me as much as they used to, and my heart felt light and no longer heavy.

Many times, a lot of us go through things that other people may not know about, and we have a heavy heart because of the burdens that we carry. I encourage you to lay all of your burdens at the altar and give it to Christ, for he *'has heard the desire and the longing of the humble and oppressed; and will prepare and strengthen and direct their hearts'* (Psalm 10:17).

God will pull you through. If he can do it for me, he can do it for you.

Five

FINAL YEAR OF UNIVERSITY

My final year of university consisted of me working two jobs, mentoring those who struggled with anxiety and depression, as well as, meeting the demands of higher education. It was a packed and busy year, to say the least. My first semester went really well, I was able to get a good balance of studying, working and socialising. However, I struggled to sleep quite a bit and would randomly wake up at 4 am almost every single day within that semester.

During the month of November 2018, I began to randomly fall into pits of sadness which I never really understood; one minute I would be fine and then the next minute I would be sad. The constant fluctuation in my mood began to irritate me, as I felt like I had no control over when it would happen, and I couldn't quite understand why it was happening either. But instead of trying to fight it, I just let it be. Whenever I fell into those pits of sadness, I just used that time to relax and to meditate rather than attempting to plough through a stressful assignment, for example, as I knew that I would become even more irritated. I believed that I would soon come out of that pit of sadness, but the feeling extended to December. As it was one of my busiest months, I didn't reside in my feelings as much as I did the previous month.

December was a month packed with assignments, exam preparation, research for my dissertation and preparation for Christmas. I decided to go home for Christmas that year even though I was, yet again, dreading it. I never felt as though we were a 'happy family' and Christmas was that one day of the year where we would play 'happy families'. We never really done anything special on the day, but we always made sure we got gifts for each other, even with the little that we had. Throughout the day everyone usually done their own thing, taking turns with the cooking every year and then coming together for dinner in the evening. Every year at Christmas, my aunty Thembi would pass by with my cousins and that was the part that I looked forward to the most, as they always brought good energy with them.

I am forever grateful to be able to celebrate Christmas, and always will be, as there are many people out there who don't get to celebrate it at all. After Christmas day it was back to the grind and within a flash, it was already new year's! I had the best entrance into the new year. As per usual, I spent it in church and the service set me up for the new year!

The first two weeks into the new year were bitter-sweet. I was joyful and hopeful about all the great things that I expected of that year, but then on the 12th January 2019, I was hit with some devastating news. I found out that my Aunty Thembi (the one who offered to take me in during the first eviction experience) had been admitted into hospital and had been diagnosed with liver cancer. My heart sank. I couldn't believe it and I genuinely had no words. I kept on thinking about Christmas day because she was experiencing pain in her stomach on that day and for as long as I can remember, she had always experienced some sort of pain in her stomach here and there. I also remember her telling me that 2018 was one of the most stressful years for her and that she never wanted to look back; so, to hear that she had been admitted into hospital was the worst news for me.

During this period, I was revising for my first set of exams for the year whilst also finishing off assignments that I had due that month. I was desperate to go to London to see my aunty as soon as my exams were done, but I had already booked a solo trip to Lanzarote, Spain, for the morning after my last exam! At the time, I thought it was the worst time for me to go on holiday as all I kept thinking about was my aunt.

But, the holiday was much more needed than I thought, and it provided me with so much clarification - the clarification that I had been longing for regarding my relationship with my mum. It was the most transformative trips that I have embarked on, as it was one where Gods voice was the clearest it had ever been to me.

Whilst I was in Lanzarote, God truly broke me apart and put me back together. This was indeed my healing period. I walked with God during my whole time there. I meditated on the beach, sang gospel melodies along the coast, journaled on the bus, and wrote letters to God whilst enjoying good meals at some great restaurants.

My time spent there was time spent with God and God alone, thus making it a place that will forever hold a special place in my heart. It was the first time that I fully addressed my biggest fear of being afraid of being loved, and the more time I spent breaking it down with God, the more clarity I gained. I began to ask myself exactly what it was that I wanted, in regard to my relationship with my mum, as it was evident that I didn't actually know what I wanted.

One question I asked myself was: What is in my control that I could change? I think so often we tend to channel our energy toward things that are out of our control and so often it tends to frustrate us rather than benefit us. It would be more beneficial if we were to channel our energy towards the things that we can control. So, I came up with a list of things that I had some sort of control over, particularly in regard to my relationship with my mum. Below are some examples that I came up with I can control:

1. The way that I respond to my mum
2. The way that I handle situations that occur within the home or regarding the house

3. Implementing healthy boundaries with my mum
4. What I decide to talk to my mum about
5. The way in which I show my mum that I love her

One thing I realised is that I was intentional about not talking to my mum about certain things, because she would so often find a way to bring religion into the conversation, and sometimes I didn't want that. I just wanted to have a normal conversation without having to feel like my mother was preaching to me. I felt like I couldn't even express myself within my own home. If I were to say something small such as, "I'm tired", she would respond with "You're not tired in Jesus name!" If I were to tell her that I don't feel well or that I'm in pain, she would jump straight into prayer.

Prayer was the answer to everything in my house. This gave me no sense of comfort, so instead of being open with her, I began to conceal things from her. Things that would be considered as normal life events to some, would be considered as an attack from the enemy to her. It was just constant negativity that I didn't want around me. So, I made the decision to be intentional about starting conversations with her that allowed little room for religious scope, but this meant that the conversations we had were very limited, thus allowing no room for our relationship to develop.

I also realised that for a very long time I had been ignoring the other ways in which my mum showed me that she loved me deeply. For example, she always spoke highly of me and my future; she has always believed in me and never doubted me. She prayed for me even when I was unable to pray for myself and she wanted the best for me, as she did for all of her children.

I was so fixated on the past hurt she had caused me that I never focused on the love she was continuously showing me. It made me realise that people show love in different ways and although I may not agree with some of the decisions that she made, I couldn't deny the fact that she did love me. It was only when I had shifted my perception that I came to that realisation. Shift your perception and see what new things you discover. Whilst reflecting on the beach, I realised that the one thing that I had struggled to let go of was the day that my mum left me with 'take care'. But now that I think about it, at least she left me with take care as there are a lot of other parents out there who have done much worse. Some parents even kick their children out onto the streets and show absolutely no remorse.

My time in Lanzarote gifted me with the opportunity to take the necessary steps to heal and to forgive. I wrote down everything that I love about my mum, everything that I love about myself, the ways in which I could love myself more and the ways in which I could show more love towards my mum.

This trip made me delve deep within myself. It made me analyse my character. It made me ask: what about me? What could I have done differently? How did my actions affect those around me? Sometimes it's so easy to focus on the other person and the wrongdoings they have done; or the hurt they have caused, that we often forget to analyse ourselves and the part that we played.

Within those five days, God made me focus completely on me. I became still, and I let God speak. I took full responsibility for the way that I spoke to my mum when I was younger and apologised.

At the time, my mum never even knew that I was abroad, none of my family did other than my sister, but there was one day where I was sat on the rocks by the coast listening to gospel music and I suddenly felt an urge to call my mum. I didn't really want to call her because I didn't want to tell her why I went on holiday and quite frankly, I didn't want to share the experience with her. So, I asked God for a sign and within a matter of seconds the clouds parted, and the sun appeared directly on me.

It was a cloudy dull day and out of nowhere a beam of sun appeared and was aimed directly at me. I still didn't call her, but the sun went and came three times! Imagine someone flashing a torchlight at you in the dark, and they turn it off and on three times. This moment was literally like that! The last time it happened I knew it was something that I had to do, so I called her and asked if she was busy and she told me that she had just come from visiting my aunt at the hospital. I told her that I was abroad and explained why I was there and why I didn't tell her beforehand.

I also told her everything that God had revealed to me during my time in Lanzarote and for the first time ever, I apologised for the role that I played in our relationship going downhill. I apologised for the way that I spoke to her during my early teenage years and I expressed that I wanted a better relationship with her. I told her all the reasons as to why I love her and commended her for her strength and ability to continue on with life after all that she had been through.

She raised us as a single mother and that is something that I appreciate a lot, so I let that be known to her.
I communicated across my needs and expressed that I didn't want someone to govern my relationship with God, and that I would appreciate it if she would just trust me, as I was always extremely intentional about developing my relationship with God.

I reminded her that it wasn't through her or because of her that I gave my life to Christ; I made that decision for myself. I also explained how hurt I was from the first housing situation when social services were called and how I felt as though I was never able to fully move on because every time I have tried to talk about the past she just dismissed me. I explained that I am an open person who loves talking about things as I believe that communication is key and that I didn't appreciate being denied the opportunity to talk about what I deemed to be necessary - particularly things concerning me.

I also communicated across how I would love for her to become an active listener - to listen with the intent of understanding rather than just listening for the sake of it. I told her that I felt as though she didn't care and that all these years have gone by and she has never apologised for any of the pain that she has caused. It was as if she was oblivious to the fact that her actions affected those around her.

At first, she tried to deflect it by saying that I should always release things to God, and that it is good that I have a relationship with God; but I told her that I had been doing that for the past several years and that it took me all that time to realise that she is the person that I needed to release all of this to. She is the one who hurt me, not God.

I needed her to know that so that I could move on and she respected that and apologised. She also said that she was really depressed during the first housing situation and so she wasn't in the right state of mind. She explained that she never ever wants me to feel like she doesn't love me because she does, hence why she named me Ntando (which means love), as when my dad left her whilst she was pregnant with me, she felt love through me. Within that moment of time, for the first time ever, she apologised. It was a very emotional moment and it is a moment that I will mark for the rest of my life, as it was at that moment that I gained closure.

My remaining days in Lanzarote were the most peaceful days I had had in a long time, and I brought that peace back with me to the UK. As soon as I landed back in London, I took a train straight to Southampton and began catching up on all the work that I had missed out on. I spent most of my days either at home studying or in the library studying, but there was this one day where I was in the library and my Aunty and my cousins were constantly on my mind.

To be exact, it was on the 13th February 2019. Whilst walking home, I decided to call my cousin to check how both him and his brother were holding up and also to see how his mum was doing. He told me that the doctors had said that my aunty only has a couple of months left to live and that if I can, I should come and see her soon. I had told him that I intended on coming down to London that weekend to see her, but as soon as I got home that day, I started to feel physically sick.

My heart was heavy, and my stomach would not stop turning. I knew then that I had to go to London immediately, so I did. I booked my ticket on that same day and left within the next hour. I felt so sick that my friend even walked with me to the coach station. On the coach, I found myself writing something that almost felt like a goodbye and I was not ready to say goodbye to my aunt.

My heart felt heavier than it had ever felt before, so I just had to release - writing is my form of release. I got home late that day, so I couldn't go to the hospital to see her, but the following morning my mum and I walked to the hospital.

On the way there we kept on talking about my aunty. I remember my mum saying that she has faith that my aunty will survive this and that God heals. She started talking about the different miracles written in the bible and the different parables concerning Jesus healing the sick, and although I couldn't dispute anything she was saying, the only thing that kept on going through my mind was that God's will is God's will - and those were the exact words that came out of my mouth. It was as if my gut was telling me that she might not make it, but my heart was crying out praying that God preserves her.

My heart completely dropped upon my entry into the hospital room that my Aunty was staying in. Never in my life had I seen my aunty in that state and to say that seeing her like that broke my heart would be an understatement. I had no words, the things that I wanted to say were replaced with endless streams of tears.

That same day my Aunty was meant to be going back home, so preparations were being made accordingly. I went with my younger cousin back to their house so that I could see my older cousin before my aunt's arrival back at her home. It was my only chance to speak to him properly to see how he was coping and how he was truly feeling. All I remembered him saying was *"I just want her to come home so that I can tell her to fight"* and that was all I needed to hear to understand how much pain he was feeling. I spent most of the day with him just talking about my Aunty and all the memories we've had, how strong she was and about how much we knew she could overcome this, given all that she had previously overcome. An hour later my cousin gets a call from our other cousin, saying, *"Put your shoes on, I'm coming to the house now so be ready"* and then she cut the phone. I was not only baffled but also scared because she left us in suspense and I could only imagine the worst to have happened.

Upon her arrival at the house, she calls us all downstairs and tells us that we have to be strong, that the doctors told her that my Aunty is no longer coming to the house and that she has a matter of hours to live rather than a matter of weeks. How did it go from her having weeks to live to hours? How did that make any sense? I didn't understand it. Everyone's emotions were high to say the very least.

In the car ride to the hospital, my cousins and I were sat in the back seat holding each other's hands and praying. I was praying that God would make a way and that he wouldn't take my Aunty from us so soon.

It had always just been my Aunty and her two boys. She raised them alone and she did an amazing job at it too, they are the most caring and loving people I know. Their mum has always been their world and she loved them more than life itself. Losing her would destroy them. We all rushed into the hospital and sat with her, talking to her the whole time, expressing just how much we loved her. For the most part of it, I couldn't even talk, I was too overwhelmed with what I was witnessing.

I was still in shock that she was in hospital, yet alone the fact that this was her last day to live. I sat right beside her, holding her hand, sending silent prayers to the Lord asking him to preserve her. We were there for hours, and most of the family had been called to come and say their goodbyes.

At one point, most of my family members had gone to get hot drinks so it was just us young ones left in the room. My Aunty wanted to stretch so me and her sons helped her do that, with each of us on either side of her.

Once we sat her back down on the bed, we sat beside her - my cousin on her left side and I on the right side of her, in order to support her. All of a sudden, she started coughing. We thought this was good at first, but then she started coughing blood. The coughing stopped, and blood just started flowing out of her mouth effortlessly. My younger sister, Kimberley, was getting sick bowls, switching them over as each got filled with blood. My cousin was screaming for a doctor as we thought that what we were witnessing was not right. We couldn't control the flow of blood that she was releasing, and it was going everywhere. Suddenly, my Aunty stopped moving but the blood was still coming out of her nose. We knew then that we had lost her.

Losing my aunt made me realise just how short life is. It actually made me value family more and made me value life more. Tomorrow really isn't promised, so remain grateful every single day and find gratitude even within the midst of a storm.

Question: are you forgiving? I find it funny how God taught me about forgiveness just before I lost someone so dear and near to me. Are you continuing to go through chapters in your life without forgiveness in your heart? Are you still holding onto past pain and hurt? If so, I urge you to reconsider forgiveness.

For those of you who have come from broken homes, make the most out of the situation you have been placed in. Be thankful for all that you have, find joy in the small things and spend time with loved ones because, just like that, the fight was over. She had gone. My younger cousin dropped to his knees and was screaming *"pleaseee nooo, pleasseeee."* He was completely broken. When he got up he started punching walls, and he had to be taken out of the room. My heart aches even writing this because I remember that day so clearly and it broke my heart witnessing how broken my cousins were.

Today I leave this message for them:

To my dearest cousins,

My eyes tear up every time I think about your mum. It still doesn't feel real to me, but she will forever hold a special place in my heart. Every time I am with you both, I am amazed by how well you are doing. I rest assured knowing that her love is so near and dear to you – it will never leave you. One thing I will never lose sight of is the pure love that she had for you both. You were her WORLD. To love is to live. Rest knowing that you were and still are deeply loved. My prayer to you both is for you to find and hold onto inner peace, for you to give life your ALL, and for you to freely give and receive love just as your mother did. I love you both deeply and wish nothing but the best for you. Know that God is always watching over you – he knows your beginning to end, so draw near to him even when you don't understand the road he's taking you down. Trust and acknowledge him in all your ways and know that once the pieces are all put together, the final picture will be beautiful. Hold on to the memories, cherish the good times and live out the good that was in her through you.

Your mum left her legacy, it's time to ensure that you leave yours.

Keep rising and never stop shining. Remember that life cannot deny itself to the person who gives life their all.

I love you both endlessly,

Your dearest cousin,

Amy xo

Tears flooded the room as other family members entered the room and saw that my aunty had passed away, as she was a beam of light in our family. Witnessing my aunty pass away scarred me and after that day, things just got harder. The funeral came around quickly and before I knew it I was back in Southampton writing my dissertation. On the day of the funeral I gave a short speech for my Aunty that read:

28/02/2019

Aunt Thembi,

She was the life of the party and the bridge that brought us all together. I think I speak on behalf of everyone here in saying that she was the most hardworking individual that I have come across and she was a true demonstration of what inner strength entails. I know that there is a time to live and a time to go, but this is by far one of the greatest losses that I have experienced. What I loved about Aunty Thembi is that she loved everyone, she loved her family and she never forgot anyone. Nobody was left out. Every Christmas she would pass by and see us, and on her arrival, she would tell me to go and get my makeup so that I could do her makeup for her. She always had a story to tell and she always had joy to bring. One thing I am sure of is that she is resting in perfect peace and I know that she would want us all to continue her legacy of being FULL OF LIFE because that is what she was. She was full of life, she loved life, but most of all she loved her two boys and I hope to reciprocate the love that she so effortlessly gave. I love you Aunt Thembi, you will never be forgotten. Rest in perfect peace.

Lots of love, Amy xo

The day after we put my Aunty to rest, I went straight back to Southampton to catch up on deadlines. It felt as though my life was going at 100 miles per hour, and all that I had witnessed within the previous two weeks still felt so surreal. One minute I was in Spain, then Southampton, then I was in London, then back to Southampton and so forth. My friends were so supportive and always told me to take time out if I needed it and I am forever grateful for them, but I have always been one to keep on going even in the midst of pain. I did my best to keep on top of my work but there were also days where I just had no energy to do anything.

The months ahead were filled with sleepless nights as I kept on having flashbacks to the moment she passed away. I kept on having dreams about death and every day I would wake up at 4 a.m. because of how intense the dreams were. Everything still seemed so surreal. There were days where I felt like everything had been taken out of me and all I could do was cry. I knew I had to release the pain rather than holding onto it, so I decided to do my own private goodbye to my aunty. I went to card factory and bought three separate helium balloons to represent: full of life. One balloon for each word. I took them to a park nearby and wrote a final goodbye speech to my aunt. As I finished reading it out loud, I released the balloons into the air and cried. I sat in the park for a while and just cried. I was so sad, and I knew that I had to release the tears, so I did just that.

A month after my aunt had passed away I still felt numb, but I kept on going. I still went to work and to university and I still kept on top of my workload. However, every weekend I found myself wanting an alcoholic drink. There wasn't a weekend in March where I didn't have an alcoholic drink and it wasn't like I just wanted a drink, it became more of a situation where I needed a drink, which wasn't normally the case.

That feeling of needing a drink soon turned into needing a cigarette and I hated cigarettes, yet I wanted one so bad, due to the built-up stress. I knew, internally, that smoking would not solve anything and the fact that I had acted upon my thoughts made me realise that I needed to deal with whatever it was that I was feeling. I didn't even get halfway through the pack before deciding to run to God instead of running from him and running towards worldly things that would not provide a long-term solution to my situation. I knew better than this.

I had experienced too many adversities in my life and each time I knew that worldly desires would not help me in any way shape or form, so instead, I decided to fully seek God. Within this season I learnt to wait on God, to lean on him, to confide in him.

Even though I didn't believe that it was my aunties time to go, I stopped questioning God and instead, I found comfort in him. I've realised that sometimes in life when you go looking for answers you won't find them, but when you shift your focus the answers come and bit by bit you begin to understand the lesson in the trial. **Life is like a puzzle; each piece has its own event but eventually, when placed together, the overall picture makes sense.**

Fast-forward to the end of my university journey, I graduated with a first-class honours degree in Sociology and Social Policy. All the praise goes to the maker! Despite all that I had experienced over the years, and particularly within my final year, I was still able to come out on top! My time at university was the most challenging but grounding experience.

Never did I think I would see my darkest but brightest days within the space of three years. I didn't just persevere for myself, but I persevered for others, for my family and particularly for the ethnic minority community.

I did it for those who continue to push themselves and put themselves out there even when all the odds are against them.

For those who are prejudged and made to feel as though they are not good enough.

For those who are thrown into a system dominated by middle-class values and forced to adapt.

For those who have to take on external responsibilities whilst balancing the demands of higher education, and for those who don't receive nearly as enough support as others - both financially and emotionally.

It wasn't just about me; it was about **US**.

On my graduation day, I came as one but represented a thousand. I will forever be passionate about changing the narrative for the ethnic minority community.

I have been gracefully broken and gracefully put back together. I have found wholeness in Christ and I hope that you can also find something of that sort. I hope that this short story of my lived experiences gives you hope in situations that may outwardly appear to be hopeless. Remember that the bible says that *'before he formed you he knew you'*, therefore *'count it all joy when you go through trials and tribulations'* because Jesus, who said that he will never leave, nor forsake you, will show up in the midst of the storm (James 1:2). My faith sustained me through it all and I will forever be grateful. Keep your head up high and fight the good fight of faith.

THIS IS JUST THE BEGINNING.

PART 2

PRIORITISING PROGRESSION
AND

AVOIDING STAGNATION

The next section of this book will encapsulate some of the most crucial things that I have learned throughout my journey in life, thus far.

It will capture the practical steps that I have taken to heal and to continue moving forward in life, even within the midst of a storm.

Just to be clear, the practical steps that I have taken have worked for me and this is not to say that they will work for everyone, but they could work for you if you are open-minded enough to try them.

As I invite a fresh perspective into your life, I urge you to read and receive all that I have written with both an open mind and heart.

Throughout the next two chapters, there will be questions for you to consider, so I encourage you to take the necessary time out to give your undivided attention to these questions and to answer them, in-depth, to the best of your ability. These questions are all about YOU. They will help you delve deep within yourself, to fully discover and understand who you are.

The key is to first discover your true identity and then your capabilities. Some of the tips that I give are embedded within the text and are not written out as point-blank steps to be taken away and may, therefore, not seem evident; so, when you read this section, read it intently.

It is important to remember that this is just a foundation that I am laying down for you - it is just a starting point. The rest of the work is down to you. Do you want to continue progressing or do you want to remain stagnant? You choose.

Six

YOU CHOOSE

In every life there is a choice. A choice to keep on moving or a choice to stand still. Do not undermine the power that lies within.

South Africa, Cape town, Summer 2018.

'Pain is temporary. Quitting lasts forever.'

LANCE ARMSTRONG.

Embracing pain does not mean standing still

There are those who are faced with some of the most tragic adversities in life, yet they still seem to manoeuvre their way through life as if they have had every advantage in the world. Then there are those who experience similar hardships, but their response occupies the back seat rather than the driver's seat. For those of you who tend to find yourself in the position of the back seat, this chapter is here to let you know that you can embrace pain whilst still moving forward in life.

This is not to say that you should not take the time to sit with your pain/struggle, but that you must pick yourself back up and keep moving.

The space between pain and wholeness deserves your undivided attention. It will require both patience and presence of mind, and with presence of mind comes stillness - but you must distinguish between when stillness is beneficial and when it can be harmful.

Practising stillness is good when used as a process of decluttering your mind, helping you to empty your thoughts and reselect the beneficial ones. It is good when it's used as a way to delve deep within yourself, to analyse your character - both the good and the bad - and then to decide which aspects of yourself can stay and what needs to go. Use stillness to pay attention to your thoughts, feelings and needs, with the aim to understand their value.

Elizabeth Gilbert put it perfectly when she said, *"By feeling your own feelings you open up your feelings more universally to the world."* Stillness is good when it helps you refine your goals, your vision and your passion. It's beneficial when used to sit-down with yourself and become one with yourself. Listen to your heart, to your intuition or to God.

Use stillness to connect the threads that have been lost in a disconnected world, and to gain guidance and clarity.

The only way through is through, so step into it, feel through it and heal through it. But be aware as to when stillness can be harmful. Tell me if this sounds like you:

> *You are in a bad place both physically, spiritually and mentally and you can't seem to get out of your head. Your mind is cluttered and instead of trying to de-clutter it, you reside in your thoughts – thoughts that are unhealthy. Without even realising it, you dig yourself an even deeper hole and then eventually you become numb and are no longer in touch with yourself. This is when things can become dangerous because you no longer feel. Instead, you allow other people's thoughts and opinions to govern you – to govern your thoughts, your beliefs and even your feelings. Instead of attempting to discover what the root cause is for yourself, you believe what other people tell you it is. You no longer pay attention to what your body*

needs, but instead you pay attention to the voices of others. You listen to others more than you listen to your intuition. You listen to others more than you listen to your soul. You listen to others more than you listen to God. That is when stillness can be harmful.

You must do all that you can to avoid this state of being. If you want to cry, **cry standing up**. Stand tall with your head held high, knowing that you have the ability to rise above the challenge, and to rise above the pain.

You may not believe that you have the ability to rise above it within that given moment of time, but think of all the times you have risen above other things. Consider for a moment just how resilient you are.

The trials that you face in life are not meant to stop you but are there to help move you towards your divine destiny. Pain is an inevitable part of life and the sooner you accept that, the better. Through acceptance, you give yourself permission to feel the pain, acknowledge it, embrace it and rise above it.

For those of you who may be thinking that this is much easier said than done - especially given the many situations that are out of your control - I feel you. However, what you can control is your ability to channel the inner strength that lies within you, as embracing pain whilst still moving essentially boils down to how well you activate the power that lies within.

We only get a one-way ticket to this ride called life, so you have to play your cards right. You can either continuously pull out the self-pity card or you can pull out the 'I am an overcomer' card - you choose.

There have been many times in my life where I got up in spite of opposition because it is my responsibility and mine alone, to show up for myself every day regardless of the challenge.

I know that life can be hard, as mentioned previously, I have had my fair share of trials and I will continue to be presented with obstacles, all of us will; but what matters is how you handle what is thrown your way. You have to learn to be in action and be accountable even when it's uncomfortable.

Discomfort is what leads to growth, so be encouraged when you are placed in uncomfortable situations.

Consider these three essential steps that will enable you to embrace pain whilst continuously moving:

1. **Find a foundation that is anchored in something other than your emotions, as your emotions will continuously fluctuate.**

Your foundation should keep you upright. It should equip you to grow through your most difficult seasons and sustain you. My foundation is Christ. In the middle of my storms and in the middle of my trials I have learned to fix my eyes on Jesus and be still. I have continuously put my faith in God and he has never let me down. He is my anchor to the ground, my hope and my firm foundation. I have held onto my faith even in the darkest of moments and have continuously persevered. Where you think your solution is, is where you will put your faith, so make sure you are putting your faith in the right thing otherwise it will destroy your faith.

For those of you who may be wondering how to find your foundation - ask yourself these essential questions:

o What will edify you?

o What will help mould you into the best version of yourself but will never change?

   - For example, reading the Bible helped mould me into the person that I am today, and I know that I can always run back to it, as God's word will never change.

o What can you turn to/run to that will always be there?

   - For example, I always turn to God as I know that he will always be there. He will never leave me nor forsake me.

o What will keep you upright?

o What **truth** will pull you through?

The truth that pulls me through lies within the scripture, John 3:16, which says: 'For God so loved the world that he gave his only begotten son, that whosoever believeth in him shall not perish but shall have everlasting life'. I rest knowing that God loves me too much to ever forsake me. He gave up his only begotten son to die on the cross for my sins, so that I may live. There's no other purity of love than the love of God. His love keeps me upright and his word edifies me.

2. Believe that YOU hold the power to change your situation.

What you believe will form the basis of your thoughts, which will in turn affect your actions as 'thought is cause and experience is effect'. To take responsibility for your life is to take responsibility for your thoughts. So, if you believe that you hold the power to change your situation, then this will form the basis of your thoughts and will cause you to act accordingly. You will always behave in a way that is consistent with the way that you see yourself. So, if you are not behaving in a way that will allow you to bring out the good in a situation that may outwardly appear to be bad, then you need to change the way that you see yourself. See yourself as someone more than capable, someone who is powerful, someone who is worthy and someone who is loved. For you to change the way you see yourself, you have to change your thoughts. For some of you, you may have to transform your mind to think of 'whatever is true, whatever is right and confirmed by Gods word, whatever is pure, whatever is wholesome, and whatever brings peace' (Philippians 4:8).

Questions to consider:

o   How do you see yourself?

o   What consumes your mind?

o   Are your thoughts benefitting you or costing you?

o   How are you building your mental muscle?

o   What good can you see in a situation that may outwardly appear to be bad?

3. Make the conscious decision to keep going no matter the odds.

Consider these two steps that will help you make the decision to keep on going no matter the odds:

1.   Know your why. Ask yourself: Why should I keep on going? Why is it absolutely crucial that I pull through?

2.   Have a vision and refine it.

The two intertwine. Knowing your why will help pull you through some of your toughest moments and your motivation will be your vision. Learn to live out of your vision as it is more powerful than living out of your circumstance. Your vision is what makes all things meaningful, it makes pain meaningful. Acknowledge where you have been, what you have experienced, what you have felt and then shift your focus towards where you want to be, what you want to experience, and what you want to feel. Life will test your vision but even in the midst of the pain, and amid the challenges, you must hold onto your vision. Some of the greatest people in history have held onto their vision in the midst of affliction and opposition. For example, if we take a look at Martin Luther King – a social activist who played a key role in the American civil rights movement - we can see how willing he was to endure constant oppositions - ranging from street attacks to home bombings - in order to see his vision of a society where people are no longer judged, according to the colour of their skin, come into fruition. Another great example would be Nelson Mandela - an anti-apartheid revolutionary, an impeccable leader and philanthropist who served as President of South Africa from 1994 to 1999. He fought for those who were divided by the system of racial segregation and endured twenty-seven years in prison to see his vision come to pass. He lived out of his vision even whilst in solitary confinement and refused to succumb to despair. Solitary confinement alone is considered to be home to detrimental phycological effects on individuals, so his ability to survive all that he encountered, shines light to how both his determination and perception were undiminished.

Your motivation will always be in direct proportion to your expectation. So, know your end goal, exercise your will power accordingly and keep on going.

Questions to consider regarding your vision:

o Do you have a vision?

o Have you written your vision down?

o Do you believe in your vision?

- You will only be able to implement as much as you feel and believe is possible.

o Do you throw your vision over every obstacle?

o How are you currently working towards your vision?

- What is the smallest action that you can take to make progress toward your vision?
- *Action is the antidote to despair*
                                        (Joan Baez)

o Will you allow your vision to motivate you or to overwhelm you?

- *Where motivation meets method is where implementation begins.*
-

Hidden treasures in the darkness

'My darkest moments have been my greatest lessons.'

AMY GUDUZA.

There have been times in my life where I have been eager to run away from my struggles, and from the difficult situations that so effortlessly weighed me down. However, I soon learned to be in less of a hurry to rush away from experiences that held the potential to change my life.

I think so often, as human beings, we can be quick to find something to distract us from walking with an open mind and heart towards our most difficult and painful moments. It is within these dark moments that hidden treasures are being pulled out of us*, hence why it is absolutely crucial that we remain attentive within these seasons; and make the conscious decision to look at something just a little bit closer than we usually would.

Darkness is so often described as the absence of light*. However, it can also be described as a void or as some would like to say, an emptiness. Darkness is often experienced as an internal feeling. This feeling may be influenced or exacerbated by external factors, but it is not the external that needs to be dealt with, it is the internal. The experience of darkness is, therefore, a revelation of the absence of something.

Our darkest moments are the moments whereby our souls are crying out for attention and it is within these moments that we are required to be alert in order to grasp what our souls are missing*. What do you need to feed your soul with? There is something to take away from every situation, as every moment is giving you an opportunity to be a better you, but only you can figure out what that thing is.

Do not be afraid to dwell in your own company. Do not be afraid to look at a situation with a different lens – the lens of someone who can and will come out better and stronger. Do not be afraid to walk through all that you encounter rather than attempting to run away from it.

Our lives are our greatest teachers and one thing that my life has taught me is that: **God is not as concerned with my comfortability as he is with my correction**, so he will place me in uncomfortable situations just so that I can be corrected. I remember there was one time whereby I went through the same thing three times and I began to get frustrated. I didn't understand why that particular thing was happening and I started to get very disheartened, but through that season I realised that my attitude towards the situation had not changed; and therefore, the way that I dealt with it was quite similar to previous times.

I realised that God had placed me in those similar situations over and over again until I began to live like I had learnt the lesson that he was trying to teach me. Sometimes you have to stop looking at the situation and start looking at yourself. Ask yourself questions.

Consider asking yourself the questions below:

o   Within this current moment of time, how are you truly feeling?

o   Given all that is currently taking place, how are you managing?

o   Do you feel as though you are in a rush to get out of this season? If so, ask yourself why?

o   What do you feel like your soul needs right now?

o   What areas do you think you are lacking in?

o   What do you need to practice more of?

o   What is this experience teaching you? What can you take from it?

o   What practical steps have you set in place to help you walk freely throughout this season?

All that you have within you is all that you have to give to the world. It is therefore necessary for you to become in tune with your higher self and intuition and pay attention to what each season is teaching you. Do not let life pass you by. The most responsible thing that you can do right now is to manage the story that will be told about you when you make a transition. Recognise where you are and be your own rescue. Through it all trust your journey because what many of you will not realise is that, it is within these dark seasons that you are being developed the most.

Aforementioned, within the first section of this book, the second semester of my second year at university was one of the most difficult seasons in my life as it was the first time whereby I felt the absence of God - and believe me when I say I have never felt like that. It was the first time whereby I felt like God had fully left me, but it was also the first time whereby I sought God like never before, in ways I wouldn't have imagined.

During the beginning of that season, I allowed my circumstances to get the best of me. All that I witnessed in my immediate environment consumed my thoughts, thus resulting in me becoming stagnant. I experienced a harmful type of stillness. I allowed other people's opinions and beliefs about what I was experiencing to consume me. I actually let other people tell me how I was feeling rather than allowing myself to feel and discover the truth of my reality. Instead of activating my spiritual practice, I allowed my emotions to take over. Overthinking swallowed me. I would find myself engaging in a task, but my mind wasn't there. I was completely out of it.

However, eventually, with time, I began seeking more and more of God, even when I didn't feel like it. Most times I felt as though I was receiving nothing back from him. This was most definitely a season of wilderness for me, but what I didn't see coming was the preparation. I didn't realise how much God was preparing me for what was about to come next in my life.

As I spent more time seeking God and his word, I began to receive different revelations. God began to reveal himself to me in new ways, and it was actually through one particular song whereby I realised exactly what it was that God was trying to teach me. God had taken me to school without me even realising until the class was over! There is a saying that some people have more faith than others, however, Marianne Williamson says that a truer statement is that *'in some areas, some people are more surrendered than others'* and I couldn't have agreed anymore.

It was within this season of darkness where I learned to let God into every single area of my life. It was within this season that I realised that in some areas I trusted my own ability rather than trusting God. It was within that moment that I discovered that seasons of darkness are one of the many ways that God chooses to get your attention. Sometimes, when things are going smoothly, we become comfortable and fixated on the things that don't really matter, so God places us in the wilderness.

When God is getting ready to prepare you for the light, he places you in the dark. Darkness always precedes light and when God places you in a dark season, he's getting ready to pull something out of you that you didn't even know was within you*. Do not be discouraged because it is within the privacy of dark seasons that transformation takes place. God is building you*.

These seasons of wilderness are necessary because they are seasons of preparation, and wherever there is preparation, there is a pruning. Surrender and trust that God makes no mistakes.

My strength has heightened through every difficult moment and my approach to different situations has improved. My character has improved. I have moved out of my seasons of darkness much quicker through each cycle, as my previous experience has always equipped me for the next. How you manage the seasons you are placed in will determine whether that season is prolonged or made permanent.

Below are some tips that you can consider to help you to best manage your seasons of darkness:

1. Draw closer to God.

o Delve deep within the word of God and get to know his heart. Spend time talking to him and say a prayer. God sees your situation. *'He is close to the broken-hearted and saves those who are crushed in spirit'* (Psalm 34:18). Be vulnerable with him and let him into every detail of your life and season. Let him help you see this season through and believe that he will make a way as *'he will never leave nor forsake you'* (Hebrews 13:5).

2. Journal.

o Journaling not only helps you declutter your mind, but it can also be a means by which things are revealed to you. A lot has been revealed to me through my diary entries. Keeping diary entries has helped me tap into my true feelings within that given moment of time. Get to know yourself through your journal entries - ask yourself more and more questions.

o Write a letter to yourself concerning your current situation and allow yourself to be vulnerable within that moment. Don't conceal, heal. If you feel angry – express that within your journal entry. If you feel sad – express that. Tap into your emotions. Allow yourself to feel and give your feelings the attention that they require and then remind yourself of your ability to get through this.

3. Watch motivational videos or listen to podcasts.

o   These videos will help keep you in good spirit. Everyone faces battles over the course of their lives, so hearing other people's stories and the steps they took to come out on the other side may help you through your difficulties. There may be some videos that may relate directly to the current season that you are in and will therefore shine light to your situation. Hearing about other people's journeys serves as a reminder that: if they can do it, so can you.

4.   Practice gratitude.

o   Practising gratitude helps you see the good even in situations that may outwardly appear to be bad. Practice getting up every morning and saying: thank you.
o   Say out loud three things that you are thankful for.
o   Remain conscious of all the good things in your life.
-    *'And we know that God works all things together for the good of those who love Him, who are called according to His purpose' (Romans 8:28).*

5.   When you are ready, seek wise counsel.

o   Confide in someone that you trust, someone who is deeply rooted and grounded.

- That person may be able to help you unpack your season (in a shorter time frame) or may simply have a word for you that could carry you throughout that season.

Seasons of darkness are difficult but remember that it is these seasons that hold the potential to transform your life. It's often very easy to revert to bad habits within these seasons but I urge you to resist the temptation to.

Avoid taking one step forward and then ten steps backwards. Withstand the test. **Change is a beautiful thing, so be willing to make a habit of being in uncomfortable situations in order to grow, learn and receive**. The decision to manage your seasons well and to walk through them with wisdom, all comes down to you. It is a choice that only you can make. Be encouraged.

Scriptures relating to darkness*:

Ephesians 5:13:
But all things become visible when they are exposed by the light, for everything that becomes visible is light.

Colossians 1:13:
For he rescued us from the domain of darkness and transferred us to the kingdom of his beloved son.

John 1:5:
For the light shines in the darkness and the darkness did not comprehend it.

Genesis 1:4:
God saw that the light was good, and God separated the light from darkness.

Isaiah 42:16:
I will lead the blind by a way they do not know, in paths they do not know. I will guide them. I will make darkness into light before them and rugged places into plains. These are the things I will do, and I will not leave them undone.

Seven

BLOOM WHERE YOU ARE PLANTED

You must learn how to best walk freely in what you have been given.

Mumbai, India, August 2017.

'I have discovered my voice through all of my experiences. You must discover yours.'
AMY GUDUZA.

To bloom where you are planted is to give life your all, irrespective of the grounds from which you were rooted in. I believe that everyone has the ability to do this.

The phrase 'to give life your all' embodies many factors so I am aware that it is bound to mean different things to different people, hence why I believe it is important that you break this down for yourself. Discover exactly what it means to you and how you can live it out.

To get you thinking, this chapter will ask you two questions that are of uppermost importance in enabling you to begin making changes for the better.

The first will ask: who are you? One of the most crucial steps in being able to give life your all is to first discover who you are so that you can live out your true identity and then take the necessary steps to reach your desired outcome.

The second question will ask: how hungry are you? When you are really hungry for a shift in your life, you will choose to act on it. The level of hunger you experience will determine how quickly you choose to start making changes for the better. This section will explore what it really means to be hungry in life and what initiates/triggers that particular level of hunger. But first, let's begin with: who are you?

Who are you?

'As long as you find yourself, you'll never starve.'

SUZANNE COLLINS.

The road to discovering who you are will never be an easy or short journey, and in saying that it's probably one that will forever be ongoing. You are designing and building your identity every day. You will find that you learn the most about yourself through your experiences, and as long as this journey called life exists, you will continue to encounter different experiences. The good thing is that the sooner you discover who you are, the sooner you will be able to customise your life to make it fit you so that it reflects the person that you are.

Getting to know yourself is one of the best things that you can do, as it will allow you to make choices that will be beneficial to your personal growth. I so often hear the saying that our personal narrative is one of the few things that are currently under our control, and I couldn't have agreed more. There may be certain things that happen to us that are out of our control, but what we can control is our response to those encounters.

We are in control of what we choose to do with our experiences, particularly whether we decide to use them for the greater good. There is power in finding yourself and discovering who you are, but you must first make the decision to do so. It is a choice.

A lot of my self-discovery came from opportunities that presented themselves to me, which I did not hesitate to explore. For example, I learned a lot about myself during the twenty-one days I spent in India, in 2017, with people that I had only met with twice prior to my departure.

At the age of 19, I was exposed to a new environment, new people, a new culture, a new way of living. I became aware of what I could tolerate and what I couldn't tolerate, what my weaknesses were and what my strengths were; how to push myself and what I was passionate about. I asked people questions about myself. I wanted to see what their thoughts were about me, having known me for such a short period of time. What was I portraying to the world? What was I portraying to those who knew nothing about me? What did they think my strengths were and what my weaknesses were? What areas did they think I could improve on? This isn't to say that you must always agree with what others think of you, but that you should self-analyse through a different lens. Sometimes we tend to either only see the good in ourselves or only see the bad when essentially, we should be aiming to recognise both. Pull out your areas of improvement and work on it, but also recognise your strengths and use it to your advantage. I noticed how much I struggled with resisting the urge to carry other people's burdens as my own and just how much this weighed me down. I also noticed how much drive and potential I had within me.

One thing that I discovered was not only the importance of having weak ties but the value that it carries. I was in a completely new environment with people whom I knew nothing about, yet I learnt more from them in such a short period of time than I had from those within my close-knit community.

Engaging with new people gives you access to something fresh, whether that is a fresh perspective or a fresh opportunity. It paves a new path that only you will be able to discover where it will take you - if you are curious enough to explore it.

I was not only given the privilege of getting to know my peers, but I also worked with girls who, at the age of 14, had created apps with the hope of solving ongoing issues that they encountered within their local communities. They didn't just look out for themselves, they looked out for each other. At the age of 16, some of these girls were already in university and ahead of the game. Despite their poor living conditions and the external battles that they encountered daily, they never failed to show gratitude and emanate joy irrespective of their circumstances.

One of the girls I worked with invited my peers and I into her home, where she lived with her mother and younger sibling. Their house was probably the equivalent to the size of two bedrooms in my house in London. Their bedroom, bathroom and kitchen were all cramped up within one small room, yet they were content! Their joy was not diminished by their circumstance and that young girl was a bright student who began developing solutions to the problems she encountered within her immediate environment. That is what I call blooming where you are planted. It was an honour to spend time with them and to get to know them on a personal level.

To say that my sense of gratitude strengthened during my time in India, would purely be an understatement. My time spent in India helped me to re-evaluate and refine my values, and ever since, I have been wearing my values on my sleeve daily. **Everything you think, say and do should attest to your values and morals in life.**

It is without a doubt that a lot of my experiences have shaped who I am. However, before taking a look at my experiences, I wrote down the words that would come to mind when I thought about who I am. I went back to the basics and realised that I am a lot of things. I am a child of God, a Christian, a saved soul, a daughter, a sister, an aunt, a cousin and a friend. I am a giver, an active listener, a talker, an encourager, a learner and a searcher. I am a fighter, a writer and a source of joy. I am resilient, fearless and I am uniquely me. The list could go on. It is important to build on the words that first come to mind when you think about who you are and look deeply within yourself, because **you are much more than just the words that come to mind.**

Below I want you to write down 5 things that you believe make you who you are. When doing this, try to think of words or phrases that cannot be changed or distorted by various events:

1. ....
....
....
....
....

2. ....
....
....
....
....

3. ....
....
....
....
....

4. ....
....
....
....
....

5. ....
....
....
....
....

Once you have the discovered the basics of who you are, you must then learn to bloom where you are planted. Use opportunities that present themselves to you as a means of learning more about the person that you are.

Remain open to trying new things, meeting new people, acquiring new knowledge and asking endless questions. Whenever you are surrounded by new people, use questions as a way to learn from them. John C. Maxwell said that *'good questions inform, but great questions transform.' 'Questions are the first link in the chain of discovery and innovation.'*

I have found that the more I have worked on myself, the more my perspective and perception has shifted, which in turn has changed my actions. Shifting your perception can take you from a place of self-pity to a position of power. This shift is what will allow you to bloom where you are planted.

Your perception is everything because we believe what we perceive to be true. Therefore, your story is your perception, thus making it your truth.

Consider these three essential steps below that will assist you in your self-discovery journey:

1. Learn to love yourself

Learning how to fully love yourself will never be an easy journey, but it will most definitely be a worthwhile journey. It is important that you embark on a journey of self-love because by loving yourself, you set the foundation as to how others should love you.

Loving yourself puts you in a higher position of power as you accept you for you and will no longer need to search for acceptance elsewhere. As you become more confident in who you are, you will know what to accept and what not to accept. You will have the power to walk away from situations that no longer serve you. You will have the power to walk away from people who constantly undermine you, mistreat you and speak poorly of you. You will know what you deserve and what you do not deserve. You will be able to say enough no's and enough yes's, so that when you do say no, it is respected.

Loving yourself comes with adjustments. Your habits may have to change. Your expectations may have to change. Your standards may have to change. Your friends may have to change. You may not be able to attend to everyone else's needs as often as you used to because your needs are now a priority. You will learn to put yourself first more often. You will learn to give yourself a break more often. You will learn to listen to what your soul needs more often.

One thing that I learnt throughout my self-love journey, is that you cannot love yourself outside the source of love - which is GOD. In her book, 'In His Image', Jen Wilkins states that *'the right love of God is what enables the right love of self and others'*, as *'Gods love is an act of will.'* He gives freely without ever wondering where his love could be better spent. As he freely gives, we must also freely give - towards ourselves and towards others. Learn to freely love yourself and never ever forget that you were *'wonderfully and fearfully made'* (Psalm 139: 14).

Learning to love yourself is a process that you must unfold yourself, but one thing that I tried, which may help you, was writing myself a love note in the voice of someone who loves me. This is what I wrote:

In the voice of someone who loves you...
14/04/20

Dear Amy,

If you could see what I see, you would see that you are the gift that keeps on giving, the light that keeps on shining and the ball that keeps on rolling. You are truly a blessing. When the going gets tough, you get tougher. When the world gives you pain, you give it love. Never let your light dim, keep on revealing yourself to the world and keep on surrendering. Thank you for the endless laughter, the tears of joy, the highs and the lows, but most of all, thank you for the courage and hope.

Lots of love,
Love xo

Try writing yourself a love note and remember that you can do this as often as you like throughout the years.

Another thing that you can try, is implementing regular reality checks into either your monthly or quarterly schedule. I often use my journal to do this and some of the things I would check are my tiredness, how much rest I was giving myself, whether I had a good balance between committing to a career but also to my own personal devotions. I would also check how much time I would spend on social media and whether it was having a negative or positive effect on my mental wellbeing. The most important thing I would examine was my routine. I would check myself emotionally, spiritually, mentally and physically. I would check whether I was getting a good balance of all four areas as they are all interlinked, so if I were to push myself too much in one area, it would affect all the other areas. Try checking yourself in all four areas and then adjust where needed.

Questions to consider:

o   What does loving yourself look like?

o   How is your time spent and with who?

   -   *The people you surround yourself with are excellent mirrors as to how much or how little you love yourself (Jen Scenciro).*

o   What are your expectations and standards?
   -   This can be in regard to your career or relationships - both romantic and non-romantic. It can also be in regard to the relationship that you have with yourself and the mental or physical state that you aspire to

achieve. Do not limit yourself when it comes to answering this question, explore all possible options.

o   What do you prioritise?

o   What will you accept and what won't you accept?

o   What is absolutely non-negotiable for you?

2.   Define and Refine your values

Your values are the things that are most important to you in life. They are mostly shaped through life experiences – both yours and those around you. It is important that you learn to define and refine your values because they will carry you through life and they will remind you of your true self.

When conflict arises, how will you respond? Will you be willing to remain true to your values or will you respond in a way that does not align with your values in life? Your values should dictate how you respond to situations. Your thoughts should attest to your values. Your speech should attest to your values. Your actions should attest to your values. **Let your values be something that you live by daily.**

Questions to consider:

o   What principles do you live by?

o   What things are of high importance to you?

o   What is the standard by which your actions are based on?

3.   Be intentional with the decisions that you make

To be intentional is to be deliberate or purposeful. Being busy without a purpose is pointless. When you are intentional, you are clear about what you want to do with what's in front of you, but in order to be intentional, you must first realise that intentionality is a choice that you have to make. It is a choice that requires you to make decisions based on what's really important to you. Being intentional is important because life is all about the decisions that you make.

Most of what you get from life will be based on the decisions that you make. A lot of your experiences are a result of your decisions, so be wise with the decisions that you make, as one decision can carry a lot of weight. Moving from a position of helplessness to a position of power all lies within one decision. When making decisions, don't just think short-term, but instead, learn to think long-term. How will that one decision benefit you in the long-run? Remember that **small choices can have huge returns.**

One last thing that I want to point out is that your purpose may change within different seasons, therefore the decisions that you make should change accordingly. But, make sure that the decisions that you make are always in alignment with your values in life.

Questions to consider:

o Do the decisions you make stay true to your values/morals?

o Do the decisions you make benefit you or cost you?

o Do the decisions you make, make you a better person?

o Do the decisions you make feed your soul?

How hungry are you?

'If you don't act on life, life has a habit of acting on you. You can't have all that you want if you remain the person you are. To get more from life, you need to be more in life.'

ROBIN SHARMA.

I ask the question: 'how hungry are you?' Because I believe, that no matter where you start in life, you have the ability to achieve all that you desire to achieve. Sometimes the situation may not change, but you can if you make the conscious decision to.

There will be a point in your life where you realise that you have been everything for everyone but nothing for yourself, you have committed more to others than you have to yourself and that is what needs to change.

I remember getting to the stage in my life where I was tired of continuously doing things for other people and putting their needs before mine. I decided to never stop working on myself, as my personal development is the most important thing because a stronger me is a better me. You must commit to yourself and realise that in a world where everything is made available to you, you are your greatest limitation. Each and every one of us has the capacity to aspire to something, whether that's to be in a particular career or to be in a different state mentally or physically – whatever it is, you have the ability to achieve it.

Dare to ask yourself the questions that really matter in life. The ones that will urge you to act on life. What current state are you in now? What state would you like to be in? How do you feel internally? How would you like to feel internally? What do you enjoy doing? What are you passionate about? How can your talents and gifts be used for the better good of everyone? How can you serve others?

In order to breakdown what it means to be hungry, I am going to start with an analogy of food. There have been many moments in my life where I have gone hours without eating, but the point at which I would realise how hungry I am, would be when I would hear my stomach making growling noises. My stomach would be twisting and turning, and it would be within that given moment of time where I would realise just how empty my stomach was. It's within that moment where I would have to decide what to eat, as I am in control of choosing what to fill myself with. We all have certain cravings in given moments of time and we would choose that which would satisfy us and fulfil our cravings. The same applies to life.

When you are really hungry in life, it's usually because you feel empty or because something is missing from your life. This is the point where you really want more from life and you need to be filled. But the question is, what will you choose to fill yourself with? The main difference between the two types of hunger is that when making a choice regarding your soul, you must choose that which will fulfil and sustain you in the long-run. This is where intentionality comes into play. It's important that you are intentional with the decision that you make because you will bear fruits (bad or good) based on the decision that you make.

I look back at the conversations that I have had with a lot of different people and one thing that I have noticed is that it's so easy for us to complain about feeling incomplete, but when it comes down to pulling ourselves out of these situations, how consistent are we? There may be points in our lives where we may think that we have tried everything to get ourselves out of that situation but have we really? It all comes down to how much you really want to get yourself out of that state.

You must analyse what you are filling your life with and what you run to when you are longing for the feeling of completion. Analyse what you are giving your time to and make some readjustments.

Les Brown, one of the greatest motivational speakers known to date, explains in one of his speeches that when you are not filling your life with the things that you are capable of doing, then there will be gaps in your life.

When you are not living out of your true identity, then you will begin to fill those incomplete areas with things that will not even help you out of that feeling of emptiness - e.g.

taking drugs or abusing alcohol. The key is to first discover your true identity and then your capabilities.

Not only have I witnessed people around me fill their lives with unbeneficial things, but I am also a living testimony of this. Aforementioned within my story, when I was around the age of 16, I started smoking weed and drinking alcohol. I loved the feeling that smoking weed gave me as I felt like I was in another world, one that was completely different from the reality of my own.

My home was somewhere that I didn't want to be, it was somewhere that I would run from rather than run to, and instead of actually dealing with my internal feelings, I suppressed them through drinking and smoking.

Little did I know that these things were just making things worse for me. They were a distraction. A huge one. It was only until I got to a stage in my life where I realised that none of these things were fulfilling me that I decided that I wanted more from life! I was sick and tired of living that way, I was tired of constantly being a ball of happiness and energy to others but not to myself. I was tired of the endless tears, the overthinking, the anxiety, the depression, the financial deprivation, and most definitely tired of feeling unworthy of love.

Julia Quinn, a superb novelist, once said *that 'in every life, there is a turning point. A moment so tremendous, so sharp and clear that one feels as if one's been hit in the chest, all the breath knocked out, and one knows, absolutely knows without the merest hint of a shadow of a doubt that one's life will never be the same'.* For me, this turning point came when I laid my life on the altar and gave my life to Christ. I knew then that my life would never be the same. I had made the conscious decision to be responsible for my life and to do all that I could to get myself out of the bad mental state that I was in.

When I dedicated my life to Christ and started hearing more of God's word, I became hungry. I became hungry for a change. I wanted my character to be more like Christ and I wanted to do more with my life.

All of a sudden, my life had a meaning. I knew that I had so much more to give to the world and that I wouldn't be able to fulfil my purpose if I continued down the path I was headed in, so I decided to create a new garden for myself. I needed to be rooted in new soil so that the branches that I would grow would not wither. I was at a point in my life where things were falling apart but I still showed up for myself daily. I was still planting seeds even in the wilderness. I listened to sermons day in and day out. *Hunger.* Any spare moments I had were used to fill my spirit with Gods word. *Hunger.* My bedroom walls were covered in all of my sermon notes. *Hunger.* I was surrounded by his word always. I was watering my new garden with living water - the word of God. The bible says, *'blessed are those who thirst and hunger for they shall be filled'* (Matthew 5:6). I was hungry for a shift in my life, so I did not stop filling myself with the word of God and I was most definitely filled.

Rooting yourself takes time and patience, but in order to bloom where you are planted, you must have a certain type of hunger. Hunger was what I lived and breathed. This was bigger than hope, this was about my life! You have to get to a point in your life where you are sick and tired of the way that things are going for you, and you have to decide that you want more from life! It is only at this point where things will really start to shift for you as you begin chasing your dreams.

There have been many points in my life where I have been hungry for more, but particularly hungry for an internal shift.

Throughout life, I have learnt that it is our internal state that determines our experiences, not the other way around. I figured that if I could be internally peaceful and happy then everything thing else on the outside would eventually fall into place. I say this because when you are internally peaceful and happy, that is when you are most in touch with yourself, therefore granting you the power to be your best and put your best out into the world.

What you give is what you will attract. If you release positive energy you will attract positive energy and vice versa. When you are most in touch with yourself you also begin to welcome a fresh perspective with open arms.

If we take a look at some of the greatest speakers known on this earth, whether that be Lisa Nichols, Oprah Winfrey, or Les Brown, we notice how all of these people started building their vision from the soil that they were planted in. You must do the same. Success doesn't come overnight but you must be hungry enough to keep on going even when the going gets tough. Lisa Nichols, one of my favourite Motivational Speakers, never gave up when she had less than $12 in her bank account and a baby boy to feed. *Hunger.*

She didn't give up when she couldn't afford to buy her son diapers and instead had to wrap him in a towel for two days. *Hunger.*

She didn't give up when her teacher told her that her English was so poor and recommended that she get a desk job and never speak in public. *Hunger.*

Instead, she was willing to completely die to the version of herself that she knew, in order to become the woman that she wanted to be. She cut down on her expenses, she downsized her house and she got herself an extra job in order to start creating a new life for herself. *Hunger.*

Be willing to accept that not everyone will like you, not everyone will be for you and most definitely not everyone will accept you, but none of that matters! What matters the most is whether you accept yourself.

Be willing to accept your weaknesses, your strengths, your vision, and your mission and then make a commitment to do all that you can within your power to bring your vision into reality. Face rejection in the face and keep on moving, don't stop just because of one setback or two.

The bible says 'for though the righteous fall seven times, they rise again, but the wicked stumble when calamity strikes' (Proverbs 24:16). No matter how many setbacks you get you must keep on going because your setbacks will be your greatest comebacks. Bishop T.D. Jakes states that rejection is God's way of direction and that how you handle rejection determines whether you will be successful in life. I couldn't have agreed more with this statement.

Do not give up on the vision just because of another person's response, but rather, be willing to seek criticism and analyse whether there could be room for improvement and have enough faith to bring your vision into fruition. You must also learn to define success for yourself and celebrate your successes along your journey - nothing is too small to be celebrated and behaviour that gets celebrated is behaviour that gets repeated.

What does success mean to you? What does prosperity mean to you?

Go where you have never gone before, do the things that you have never done before, make changes to your routine and be willing to take that leap of faith in order to become the man or woman that you want to be.

I envision my life every day and my past is the fuel that keeps me going. Nothing and no one can change my mind about the things I have seen in my future. I know where I have been, and I know what state I never want to be in again, and now I know where I am headed.

My self-development has been one of my main priorities for the last three years and will forever continue to be, as there is always room for improvement. One thing I worked on the most was taking a hold of my thoughts. I really invested into my mindset. I read books, watched sermons, listened to podcasts, joined different forums, attended different conferences and fellowshipped with others.

I was intentional with the decisions that I made in order to live a more fulfilled life. Being intentional is important, but this is not to say that you must completely rule out going with the flow. However, there are many errors of continuously going with the flow - one being that you may deprive yourself of the opportunity to reach your full potential. This is because if you are always going with the flow, you are unlikely to realise when it is time for you to move to the next level. You are less likely to make intentional decisions and may instead, adopt the mindset of 'whatever will be, will be'. This may cause you to prolong being in a season that God actually wants to take you out of.

You must learn to be in action and accountable even when you may not want to be. Always pay attention to the seasons that you are in and keep track of your progress. Recognise when it is time to move, when it is time to accelerate.

Questions to consider:

o What areas of your life feel empty?

o What do you want to change?

o What turnaround are you hoping for?

o What steps are you taking to become more deeply rooted?

o   Are you acting on life or are you letting life act on you?

o   Are your actions intentional or do you continuously go with the flow?

Being hungry can catapult you into fulfilling your purpose. The future belongs to those who prepare for it. Prepare for yours. Transcend your environment and throw your visualisations over every obstacle.

Life gives you two options:

1. You can map out your path and make it happen
        OR
2. You can create excuses as to why it's not possible

YOU CHOOSE.

KEY QUOTES / TAKE AWAYS

LOVE MATTERS.

You are as close to God as

you choose to be.

Learn to find and maintain gratitude, even within the midst of a storm. Find joy in the small things.

Use stillness to connect the threads that have been lost in a disconnected world and to gain guidance and clarity.

Your foundation should keep you upright. It should equip you through your most difficult seasons and sustain you.

Acknowledge where you have been,

what you have experienced,

what you have felt

and then **shift your focus** towards

where you want to be,

what you want to experience

and what you want to feel.

Your motivation will
always be in direct
proportion to your
expectation.
So, know your end goal,
exercise your will power
accordingly and keep going.

Everything you think,

say and do

should attest to your values

and morals in life.

Rooting yourself takes time

and patience,

so be patient with yourself.

As long as you find
yourself,
you'll never starve.

Suzanne Collins.

WHAT'S NEXT?

'There is nothing more tragic than to find an individual bogged down in the length of life, devoid of breadth.'

MARTIN LUTHER KING JR.

If you've made it this far, then I assume you have made it through the whole book - congratulations. How do you feel? Enlightened? Excited? Ready to embark on a new journey? I can only hope that this book will be a stepping stone for you to continue to find healing along the course of your life. All the steps that I have provided are steps that must be carried out continuously.

We all battle with something along the course of our lives, and we owe it to ourselves to continue ploughing through. I have opened up my heart up to you all and you have seen what I have battled with, but most importantly you have seen what I have overcome.

Struggling to write this book, in what many would call unprecedented times, I went through weeks of not typing a word. The battle to keep up with the demands of the world and to maintain peace of mind in a year that has been consumed by so much loss, due to a global pandemic (covid-19), has been intense. The battle to not resist external pressures and to give this book the time and attention that it deserved was tough, and this was most definitely heightened by the inability to work in a variety of places.

Working in the same place day in and day out without a change of environment was not easy. But, being stuck indoors for months without being able to socialise with others, made me realise just how grateful I am for the platforms that have been put into place for us to continue to connect with others, all across the world, digitally.

Along the way, I have realised the importance of doing small great things with joy and this book is just one of the many small great things that I will do.

I want to conclude this book with the idea that has underpinned all of what you have just read. That is, life is all about the choices that you make.

We cannot control what happens to us, but we can control our response to those situations. Will you allow the challenges of life to weigh you down or will you rise to the challenge? **To be defeated or to continuously say yes to life?** You must choose.

So, here you are at the end of this book. I guess the only question left to ask is: what's next? Your choices. What will you choose to do with all of this information? Not just now, but also moving forward. My words are not meant to just touch you, they are meant to impact you. Build on all you have gained or all that you have related with. Delve deep into your own life. Find methods that work best for you, that will allow you to continue to move forward in life and to say yes to life in spite of all the challenges that may be thrown your way. It is time for you to bloom where you have been planted!

For those of you who love reading as much as I do, I have prepared a short list of books for you to read next. These are books that have helped me along the way and have even challenged my thinking. I would like to send this to you directly, providing you with easy accessibility.

If you would like these recommendations, or equally, if you would like to discuss this one, all you have to do is email amyguduza@gmail.com

BIBLIOGRAPHY

Brown, L. (2017) *You've gotta be hungry – motivation.* [online] Youtube.com. Available at: <https://www.youtube.com/watch?v=uFBqCPj6n44&t=3s&ab_channel=TimRobins>

Gilbert, E. (2020) *It's OK To Feel Overwhelmed: Here's What To Do Next.* [online] Youtube.com. Available at: <https://www.youtube.com/watch?v=oNBvC25bxQU&t=659s&ab_channel=TED>

Jay, M. (2012) *The Defining Decade: Why Your Twenties Matter and How to Make the Most of Them Now.* Canongate Books.

Maxwell, C., J. (2014) *Good Leaders Ask Great Questions: Your Foundation for Successful Leadership.* Center Street.

Nichols, L. (2015). *Abundance Now: Amplify Your Life & Achieve Prosperity Today.* Harper Collins.

Nichols, L. (2017) *Rescuing Yourself, Overcoming Fear and Finding Success By Serving Others.* [online] Youtube.com. Available at: <https://www.youtube.com/watch?v=tSxhIp4l1DY&ab_channel=TammyGolden>

Quinn, J. (2009) *When He Was Wicked: The 2nd Epilogue.* Harper Collins.

Sincero, J. (2013) *You Are a Badass: How to Stop Doubting Your Greatness and Start Living an Awesome Life.*

Warren, R. (2002) *The Purpose Driven Life: What on earth am I here for?* 10th Edition. Zondervan.

Williamson, M. (1992) *A Return to Love: Reflections on the Principles of "A Course in Miracles".* Harper Collins.

Wilkins, J. (2018) *In His Image: 10 Ways God Calls Us to Reflect His Character.* Crossway.

ACKNOWLEDGMENTS

I am thankful that I have been able to see this book right through to the end, but I must make it clear how appreciative I am of the many authors who I gained insight from and relied on over the years. I feel incredibly grateful for the wisdom that they have shared through both their books and talks.

This book would not be what it is without the large amount of support provided by my friends and family. I want to thank my friend Ife Opedo, who not only helped me personally during the writing of this book, but was also my most dedicated reader. Thank you for your words of wisdom, for your encouragement, for your prayers and your continuous support.

I want to give a special thanks to Tatenda Madivani and Ayoduro Okuboyejo for joining me, alongside Ife Opedo, in prayer for 30 days prior to the release of this book.

I also want to thank all of my other friends who have supported my vision - you know who you are - but I particularly want to thank those who have read several sections of this book and have provided me with invaluable feedback. Thank you, Betsy Emeka, Shona Gyamfi, Ariana

Getnet, Alicia Pitchford, Rachel Robinson and a big thanks to my sister Fikile Guduza, who never failed to check how much progress I was making throughout the writing process. I also want to thank my cousin Makhosi Dlamini, for encouraging me to tell my truth.

I owe a big debt of gratitude to Kate Liverman, who provided critical notes early on that I am grateful for. Her notes were of assistance in helping me figure out a structure that would best convey both my lived experiences and my thoughts.

Finally, my biggest depth of gratitude is dedicated to God, for without him this would not have been possible. My faith has continuously sustained me throughout the challenges that life has presented me with and the strength of the Lord has carried me throughout this writing process.

SCRIPTURE INDEX

GRACEFULLY BROKEN

MY PARENTS AND I

- Psalms 139:14

HOME

- Genesis 1:26-28
- Luke 10:19
- Psalm 8:6
- Deuteronomy 31:6

THE BEGINNING OF FREEDOM

- Proverbs 4:23
- Ephesians 6:12
- Genesis 13:14
- Psalm 46:1

UNIVERSITY

1. James 1:2-8
2. Romans 8: 28
3. 1 Corinthians 13:4
4. Psalms 35:27
5. John 15:4-5
6. Matthew 6:33
7. Proverbs 9:10
8. Ecclesiastes 11:3
9. Psalm 10:17
   FINAL YEAR OF UNIVERSITY

1. James 1:2

PRIORITISING PROGRESSION AND AVOIDING STAGNATION

YOU CHOOSE

1. Philippians 4:8
2. Psalm 34:18
3. Hebrews 13:5
4. Romans 8:28
5. Ephesians 5:13
6. Colossians 1:13
7. John 1:5

Genesis 1:4
Isaiah 42:16

BLOOM WHERE YOU ARE PLANTED

Psalm 139: 14
Matthew 5:6
Proverbs 24:16

Printed in Great Britain
by Amazon

32286300R00098